D0118735

Better Homes and Gardens®

Snacks
and
Appetizers

Contents

Party Menus 104

Seventeen guest-pleasing menus for parties. Recipes and tips for
a patio party, appetizer buffet, informal get-together, open house,
afternoon tea, poker party, children's picnic, pizza party, and
other parties for large and small groups. Serving hints, table
setting ideas, and suggestions for organizing food preparation.

Index 108

On the cover: This dazzling collection of recipes includes *Pizza
Muffins, Marinated Vegetable Snack, Caramel Crunch, Turkey-
Olive Cocktail,* and *Cran-Raspberry Float.* (See index for pages.)

BETTER HOMES AND GARDENS BOOKS

Editorial Director: Don Dooley
Managing Editor: Malcolm E. Robinson   Art Director: John Berg
Asst. Managing Editor: Lawrence D. Clayton   Asst. Art Director: Randall Yontz
Food Editor: Nancy Morton
Senior Food Editor: Joyce Trollope
Associate Editors: Sharyl Heiken, Rosemary Corsiglia
Asst. Editors: Elizabeth Strait, Sandra Mapes, Catherine Penney, Elizabeth Walter
Designer: Harijs Priekulis

Our seal assures you that every recipe in *Snacks
and Appetizers* is endorsed by the Better Homes
and Gardens Test Kitchen. Each recipe is tested
for family appeal, practicality, and deliciousness.

Specialty Snacks

What foods come to mind when you think of snacks? Popcorn? Cookies? Cheese and crackers? Why not change your thinking and treat yourself, your family, or your guests to snacks that are out of the ordinary, such as tacos, soft pretzels, or homemade sherbet. These special snacks, and the other recipes in this section, give a new excitement to snacking.

Having everyone fashion their own pizza using a variety of fillings adds to the fun of a party or a family get-together. Cooking at the table is always enjoyable, especially when you're sampling a new fruit, cheese, or vegetable fondue snack. And don't overlook the home-baked breads, marinated fruit and vegetable nibbles, sandwiches, cookies, and candies in this section. Each is an unordinary treat.

Layer chicken filling, lettuce, tomato, cheese, and avocado atop fried tortillas to make *Chicken Tostadas* (see recipe, page 16). Accompany with beer served in salt-rimmed mugs. To prepare the mugs, rub the rims with cut lime, then dip in salt.

Fondue Highlights

Bring out the fondue pot for everyday snacks and for entertaining. Fondue get-togethers are convenient for the hostess and are enjoyable for everyone participating. You'll find a variety of fondue recipes on the next few pages.

Chocolate-Butter Mint Fondue

    1 14-ounce can *sweetened condensed* milk
    1 7-, 9-, or 10-ounce jar marshmallow creme
    1 6-ounce package semisweet chocolate pieces (1 cup)
    ⅓ cup crushed butter mints
    ¼ cup milk
    2 tablespoons crème de cacao
    Apple or banana dippers

In saucepan combine first 4 ingredients. Cook and stir over low heat till chocolate melts. Stir in milk and crème de cacao. Transfer to fondue pot; place over fondue burner. Spear dipper with fondue fork; dip into fondue, swirling to coat. Makes 6 to 8 servings.

Dippers to dunk in fondues

Many foods, even leftovers, make suitable and interesting fondue dippers. Cut foods into bite-size pieces and allow about 10 dippers for each person.

Dippers for sweet fondues: Fresh fruit (to keep from browning, dip in lemon juice mixed with a little water), canned fruit, angel cake, pound cake, brownies, cookies, marshmallows, and pretzels.

Dippers for other fondues: French or Italian bread (cut cubes so that each has one crust), hard rolls, breadsticks, bagels, English muffins, cooked seafood, meat, or poultry, cherry tomatoes, cooked vegetables, and fried potato nuggets.

Creamy Peach Fondue

    1 29-ounce can peach slices
    3 tablespoons sugar
    2 tablespoons cornstarch
    ¾ cup whipping cream
    1 tablespoon lemon juice
    ½ teaspoon vanilla
    ¼ teaspoon almond extract
    Pound cake, angel cake, or gingerbread dippers

Drain peaches, reserving ¼ cup liquid. In blender container combine reserved liquid and peaches. Cover; blend till smooth. In saucepan combine sugar and cornstarch; stir in peaches, cream, and lemon juice. Cook and stir till thickened and bubbly. Stir in vanilla and almond extract. Transfer to fondue pot. Place over fondue burner. Spear dipper with fondue fork. Dip in fondue; swirl to coat. Serves 6.

Pink Squirrel Fondue

    1 7-, 9-, or 10-ounce jar marshmallow creme
    3 tablespoons crème d'almond
    1 tablespoon white crème de cacao
    1 teaspoon lemon juice
    Banana or strawberry dippers

In saucepan combine marshmallow creme, crème d'almond, white crème de cacao, and lemon juice. Cook and stir over low heat till heated through, about 2 minutes. Transfer to small fondue pot; place over fondue burner. Spear dipper with fondue fork; dip into fondue, swirling to coat. Makes 4 to 6 servings.

A delicately flavored fondue snack

Plump strawberries and ripe bananas serve as tasty → dippers for *Pink Squirrel Fondue*. This sweet, creamy fondue will quickly become a snack favorite.

Quick Dessert Fondues

Tangy Lemon Fondue: In saucepan combine one 18-ounce can lemon pudding, ¾ cup dairy sour cream, and 1 teaspoon vanilla. Cook and stir over low heat till heated through. Transfer to fondue pot; place over fondue burner. Serve with gingerbread, angel cake, or fruit dippers. Makes 2½ cups.

Cinnamon-Applesauce Fondue: In saucepan combine one 16-ounce can applesauce and ¼ cup red cinnamon candies. Cook and stir over low heat till candies are dissolved and mixture is heated through. Transfer to fondue pot; place over fondue burner. Serve with fruit or angel cake dippers. Makes 2 cups.

Lemony Blueberry Fondue: In saucepan combine one 21-ounce can blueberry pie filling and one 3-ounce package lemon-flavored gelatin. Cook, stirring occasionally, till heated through. Transfer to fondue pot; place over fondue burner. Serve with pound cake or fruit dippers. Makes 2½ cups.

Maraschino Cherry Fondue: In saucepan combine one 18-ounce can vanilla pudding and ⅓ cup chopped maraschino cherries. Gradually stir in ½ cup maraschino cherry juice and ½ cup milk. Cook, stirring constantly, till heated through. Transfer pudding mixture to fondue pot; place over fondue burner. Serve with fruit dippers. Makes 3 cups.

Apricot Fondue: Spoon one 22-ounce can apricot pie filling into saucepan; snip apricots into tiny pieces. Stir in ½ cup orange marmalade, 2 tablespoons sugar, and 2 teaspoons cornstarch. Cook and stir till thickened and bubbly. Transfer to fondue pot; place over fondue burner. Serve with angel cake, pound cake, or fruit dippers. Makes 2½ cups.

Mocha Fondue: In saucepan dissolve 2 teaspoons instant coffee crystals in 1 tablespoon milk. Stir in one 18-ounce can chocolate or chocolate-fudge pudding and 1 teaspoon vanilla. Cook and stir till heated through. Stir in ¼ cup chopped walnuts. Transfer to fondue pot; place over fondue burner. Serve with ladyfinger pieces. Makes 2 cups.

Orange French-Toasted Fondue

> 1 loaf French bread
> 4 eggs
> 1 teaspoon grated orange peel (set aside)
> 1 cup orange juice
> ½ teaspoon salt
> 1½ cups sifted powdered sugar
> ½ cup butter or margarine
> 1 egg
> ¼ cup orange juice
>   Cooking oil
> 1 teaspoon salt

Cut French bread into bite-size pieces, each with one crust. Beat together 4 eggs, 1 cup orange juice, and ½ teaspoon salt. Cream together powdered sugar and butter. Beat in 1 egg and grated orange peel. Gradually add ¼ cup orange juice, beating till fluffy.

Pour cooking oil into metal fondue cooker to no more than ½ capacity or to depth of 2 inches. Heat over range to 375°. Add 1 teaspoon salt. Transfer cooker to fondue burner. Spear bread through crust with fondue fork; dip in egg mixture, letting excess drip off. Fry in hot oil till golden brown. Transfer to salad fork; dip in butter mixture. Serves 4 to 6.

Peppy Ham Fondue

> 1 cup pancake mix
> 1 tablespoon sugar
> ½ teaspoon chili powder
> ¼ teaspoon dry mustard
> ⅔ cup water
>   Cooking oil
> 2 cups fully cooked ham cut in bite-size cubes
>   Prepared mustard

Combine first 4 ingredients. Add water and beat well. Pour oil into metal fondue cooker to no more than ½ capacity or to depth of 2 inches. Heat over range to 375°. Add 1 teaspoon salt. Transfer cooker to fondue burner. Spear ham with fondue fork. Dip in batter, letting excess drip off. Fry in hot oil till golden, 1 to 2 minutes. Transfer to salad fork; dip in prepared mustard. Makes 4 servings.

Miniature Corn Dogs

　1 cup all-purpose flour
　⅔ cup yellow cornmeal
　2 tablespoons sugar
　1½ teaspoons baking powder
　1 teaspoon salt
　2 tablespoons shortening
　1 slightly beaten egg
　¾ cup milk
　　Cooking oil
　1 teaspoon salt
　1 5½-ounce package cocktail frank-
　　　furters *or* 4 frankfurters, cut in
　　　1-inch pieces
　　Prepared mustard
　　Catsup

Stir flour, cornmeal, sugar, baking powder, and 1 teaspoon salt together thoroughly. Cut in shortening till mixture resembles fine crumbs. Combine egg and milk. Add to dry ingredients; blend well. Pour cooking oil into metal fondue cooker to no more than ½ capacity or to depth of 2 inches. Heat over range to 375°. Add 1 teaspoon salt. Transfer cooker to fondue burner. Have meat at room temperature in serving bowl. Spear frank with fondue fork; twirl in shallow bowl of batter to coat. Fry in hot oil till golden, 1½ to 2 minutes. Transfer to salad fork; dip in mustard or catsup. Makes 4 servings.

Beer-Cheese Fondue

This one starts with condensed soup —

　2 11-ounce cans condensed Cheddar
　　　cheese soup
　⅓ cup beer
　1 teaspoon prepared mustard
　1 teaspoon Worcestershire sauce
　　Dash bottled hot pepper sauce
　　French bread or vegetable dippers

In small saucepan combine Cheddar cheese soup, beer, prepared mustard, Worcestershire sauce, and hot pepper sauce. Heat and stir till mixture boils. Transfer to fondue pot; place over fondue burner. Spear French bread or vegetable dipper with fondue fork; dip in fondue, swirling to coat. Makes 4 to 6 servings.

Split Pea-Cheese Fondue

Equally delicious with ham dippers —

　2 11¼-ounce cans condensed split
　　　pea with ham soup
　½ cup process cheese spread
　⅓ cup milk
　　French bread dippers
　　Milk

In saucepan combine split pea with ham soup, cheese spread, and milk. Heat through, stirring occasionally. Transfer mixture to fondue pot; place over fondue burner. Spear bread with fondue fork; dip in fondue, swirling to coat. (If necessary, thin with additional milk.) Makes 4 to 6 servings.

Fondue safety reminders

For fondues requiring hot oil, be sure to use a metal fondue cooker with a sturdy handle. Heat the oil atop the range to the specified temperature. (Use a thermometer to check the temperature.) Do not allow the oil to smoke. When transferring the cooker to the fondue burner, handle *very carefully*, as the oil is extremely hot. Set the unit on a heatproof tray or mat to protect the table from spattering oil, spills, or heat from the burner.

Vegetables take on a new dimension when covered with a crispy coating.
To make *Vegetables in Beer Batter*, dip artichokes, cauliflower, zucchini,
and green pepper in a beer-Parmesan batter, then brown in hot oil.

Crispy-Coated Chicken Fondue

    2 tablespoons instant chicken bouillon
        granules
    ¼ cup chopped onion
    ¼ cup chopped celery
    3 large chicken breasts, skinned,
        boned, and cut in bite-size pieces
    ½ cup butter or margarine, melted
        Barbecue-flavored potato chips
        and/or tortilla chips, crushed

In metal fondue cooker mix bouillon granules
and 4 cups water. Tie onion and celery in
cheesecloth bag; add to cooker. Simmer over
range 10 minutes. Remove bag. Transfer
cooker to fondue burner. Spear chicken with
fondue fork; cook in broth 1½ to 2 minutes.
Dip in butter; roll in chips. Keep butter melted
over a candle warmer. Serves 6 to 8.

Ham and Cheese Meatballs

    1 slightly beaten egg
    ½ cup soft bread crumbs
    ½ teaspoon prepared horseradish
    ½ pound fully cooked ham, ground
        (about 1½ cups)
    2 ounces mozzarella cheese, cut into
        24 ½-inch cubes
        Cooking oil

Mix first 3 ingredients and dash pepper. Add
ham; mix well. Shape about 1 rounded teaspoon ham mixture around each cheese cube.
Pour oil into metal fondue cooker to no more
than ½ capacity or to depth of 2 inches. Heat
over range to 375°. Add 1 teaspoon salt. Transfer cooker to fondue burner. Spear ham ball
with fondue fork; fry in hot oil about 1 minute.
Transfer to salad fork. Makes 24 meatballs.

Vegetables in Beer Batter

1¼ cups beer
1⅓ cups all-purpose flour
  2 tablespoons grated Parmesan cheese
  1 tablespoon snipped parsley
  1 teaspoon salt
    Dash garlic powder
  1 tablespoon olive oil *or* cooking oil
  2 beaten egg yolks
  2 stiffly beaten egg whites
    Cooking oil
  1 teaspoon salt
  1 9-ounce package frozen artichoke
      hearts, cooked and drained
  1 medium zucchini, sliced
  1 small head cauliflower, broken into
      flowerets
  1 green pepper, cut in strips

Let beer stand at room temperature till flat, about 45 minutes. Combine flour, Parmesan, parsley, 1 teaspoon salt, and garlic powder. Stir in olive oil, egg yolks, and beer; beat till smooth. Fold in egg whites. Pour cooking oil into metal fondue cooker to ½ capacity or to depth of 2 inches. Heat over range to 375°. Add 1 teaspoon salt. Transfer cooker to fondue burner. Spear vegetable with fondue fork; dip in batter. Fry in hot oil till golden, 2 to 5 minutes. Transfer to salad fork. Serves 8.

Crab-Cheese Fondue

  2 8-ounce packages cream cheese,
      softened
  2 5-ounce jars sharp process cheese
      spread
⅔ cup milk
½ teaspoon Worcestershire sauce
  2 7½-ounce cans crab meat, drained,
      flaked, and cartilage removed
    French bread dippers

In medium saucepan combine cream cheese, cheese spread, milk, and Worcestershire sauce. Cook and stir over low heat till blended. Fold in flaked crab. Heat through. Transfer to small fondue pot; place over fondue burner. Spear bread with fondue fork; dip in fondue, swirling to coat. Makes 6 to 8 servings.

Spicy Vegetable Fondue

Serve remaining broth in soup mugs —

  3 10-ounce cans hot-style
      tomato juice
  2 teaspoons instant beef
      bouillon granules
  1 teaspoon prepared horseradish
  1 teaspoon Worcestershire sauce
    Zucchini slices, fresh mushrooms,
      cauliflowerets, and/or broccoli
      buds

In metal fondue cooker combine tomato juice, bouillon granules, horseradish, and Worcestershire sauce. Heat over range to boiling. Transfer cooker to fondue burner. Spear vegetable piece with fondue fork. Cook in boiling tomato juice mixture till crisp-tender and heated through, 1 to 2 minutes.

Crunchy Meatball Fondue

½ cup finely crushed shredded wheat
    biscuits
¼ cup sour cream dip with French onion
¼ teaspoon garlic salt
    Dash pepper
½ pound ground beef
      • • •
    Cooking oil
  1 teaspoon salt
    Sour cream dip with French onion

Advance preparation: In mixing bowl combine ¼ *cup* of the finely crushed biscuits, the ¼ cup sour cream dip, garlic salt, and pepper. Add ground beef; mix well. Shape into 24 meatballs about 1 inch in diameter. Roll in the remaining finely crushed biscuits. Place on tray; cover with foil or clear plastic wrap. Refrigerate for up to 24 hours.
Before serving: Remove meatballs from refrigerator. Pour cooking oil into metal fondue cooker to no more than ½ capacity or to depth of 2 inches. Heat over range to 375°. Add 1 teaspoon salt. Transfer cooker to fondue burner. Spear meatball with fondue fork. Fry in hot oil till browned, about 1½ minutes. Transfer to salad fork; dip in sour cream dip with French onion. Makes 4 or 5 servings.

Piping-Hot Pizzas

Want a hearty snack? Have a pizza. In this section you'll find make-ahead frozen pizzas, pizza on an English muffin, fix-ups for frozen cheese pizza, and even lamb pizza.

Spicy Lamb Pizza Wedges

  1 pound ground lamb
  ¼ cup chopped green pepper
  ½ teaspoon chili powder
  ½ teaspoon salt
  ¼ teaspoon pepper
  1 8½-ounce package corn muffin mix
  1 10½-ounce can pizza sauce with
      cheese
  2 cups shredded mozzarella cheese

In skillet combine ground lamb, green pepper, chili powder, salt, and pepper. Cook till meat is brown and green pepper is tender. Drain off excess fat. Prepare corn muffin mix according to package directions; spread batter evenly in greased 12-inch pizza pan. Sprinkle meat mixture over. Pour pizza sauce with cheese over meat. Top with shredded cheese. Bake at 400° for 20 minutes. Let stand 5 minutes. Makes 4 to 6 servings.

Oriental Pizzas

  2 12-inch frozen cheese pizzas
  ½ of a 16-ounce can bean sprouts,
      drained
  1 6-ounce package frozen pea pods,
      thawed and cut up
  1 4½-ounce can shrimp, drained and
      chopped
  2 tablespoons snipped chives
      Soy sauce

Top frozen pizzas with bean sprouts, pea pods, shrimp, and snipped chives. Sprinkle with soy sauce. Place pizzas on wire racks; set racks on baking sheets. Bake according to package directions. Makes 4 to 6 servings.

Chili Pepper Pizzas

Top pizzas with all of the meats, cheeses, and vegetables, or select as many as you want—

  1 13¾-ounce package hot roll mix
  1 cup warm water (110°)
      Cooking oil
  1 10-ounce can enchilada sauce
  2 tablespoons chopped canned green
      chili peppers
  2 tablespoons chopped onion
  4 ounces bulk pork sausage, cooked
      and drained
  4 ounces sliced pepperoni
  1 2-ounce can anchovy fillets,
      drained (optional)
  1 cup shredded mozzarella cheese
  ½ cup grated Parmesan cheese
  ½ medium green pepper, sliced
  1 3-ounce can sliced mushrooms,
      drained
  ¼ cup sliced pitted ripe olives
      Snipped parsley (optional)

Prepare hot roll mix according to package directions, *except* use warm water and omit the egg. *Do not let rise.* Cut dough into four portions. With oiled hands, shape dough into any desired shape on two baking sheets. Crimp edges of dough to make a raised edge. Bake at 450° for 6 minutes. Combine enchilada sauce, green chili peppers, and chopped onion. Spread about ⅓ cup sauce mixture on each pizza. Top with meats, cheeses, and vegetables. Sprinkle with snipped parsley, if desired. Return pizzas to oven. Bake at 450° till cheese is melted and edges of dough are browned, about 8 minutes longer. Makes 4 individual pizzas.

Hot-style pizza snacks

"Extraordinary" is the word that best describes → *Chili Pepper Pizzas,* which feature sausage, cheeses, pepperoni, green pepper, mushrooms, and olives.

Giant Pizza Sandwich

An unusual, layered pizza snack—

½ pound bulk pork sausage *or* ground
   beef
1 3-ounce can sliced mushrooms,
   drained
¼ cup chopped onion
¼ cup chopped green pepper
2 tablespoons sliced pimiento-stuffed
   green olives
½ teaspoon dried oregano, crushed
   • • •
1 cup shredded mozzarella cheese
   (4 ounces)
2 12-inch frozen cheese pizzas

In medium skillet combine pork sausage or
ground beef, sliced mushrooms, onion, green
pepper, pimiento-stuffed green olives, and
oregano. Cook, stirring constantly, till meat is
browned. Drain off excess fat. Stir in ½ *cup*
of the shredded mozzarella cheese. Place one
pizza on wire rack; set rack on baking sheet.
Spoon hot meat mixture evenly over pizza.
Top with second cheese pizza, *crust side up.*
Cover with foil. Bake at 375° for 15 minutes.
Remove foil and continue baking 10 minutes
longer. Sprinkle with remaining mozzarella
cheese. Bake 5 minutes longer. Serves 6 to 8.

Pizza Muffins

Miniature pizzas shown on the cover—

4 English muffins, split and toasted
1 8-ounce can tomato sauce with onion
   Dried oregano, crushed
½ medium green pepper
1 cup diced Canadian-style bacon *or*
   fully cooked ham
1 cup shredded mozzarella cheese
   (4 ounces)

Spread toasted English muffin halves with
tomato sauce with onion; sprinkle with oregano. Thinly slice green pepper into 8 rings.
Top muffins with Canadian-style bacon or ham.
Top each with a green pepper ring. Sprinkle
with cheese. Place muffins on baking sheet.
Broil 4 inches from heat till cheese is melted,
about 4 minutes. Makes 8 pizza muffins.

Individual Ground Beef Pizzas

1 package active dry yeast
½ cup warm water (110°)
1¾ cups packaged biscuit mix
   Cooking oil
1 pound ground beef
1 15-ounce can tomato sauce
1½ teaspoons dried basil, crushed
1 teaspoon dried oregano, crushed
¼ teaspoon garlic salt
½ cup grated Parmesan cheese
½ cup shredded mozzarella cheese

Advance preparation: Soften yeast in warm
water. Add biscuit mix; beat well. Turn out
onto cloth dusted with biscuit mix; knead 3 to
5 minutes. Divide dough into six pieces. Cover;
let rest 10 minutes. Roll each piece to a 5-inch
circle. Place on greased baking sheets; crimp
edges. Brush lightly with oil. Bake at 425°
for 5 minutes. Cook beef till browned, drain
off excess fat. Combine tomato sauce, basil,
oregano, and garlic salt. Spread about ⅓ cup
sauce mixture on each crust; top with beef and
cheeses. Wrap each pizza in foil. Seal and
label. Freeze up to 2 months.
Before serving: Bake foil-wrapped pizzas at
425° for 20 minutes. Fold foil back; bake 5
minutes longer. Makes 6 individual pizzas.

Chicken-Cheese Pizzas

½ medium green pepper, sliced
1 small onion, thinly sliced
1 tablespoon cooking oil
2 12-inch frozen cheese pizzas
1 teaspoon dried oregano, crushed
2 5-ounce cans boned chicken, drained
¼ cup sliced pitted ripe olives
1 cup shredded Monterey Jack cheese
   (4 ounces)

In small skillet cook green pepper and onion
in hot oil just till tender. Sprinkle frozen
cheese pizzas with oregano. Top with chicken,
green pepper-onion mixture, and ripe olives.
Sprinkle with shredded Monterey Jack cheese.
Place each pizza on a wire rack; set rack on
baking sheet. Bake pizzas according to package directions. Makes 4 to 6 servings.

Easy Mexican Pizza

1 package active dry yeast
½ cup warm water (110°)
1¾ cups packaged biscuit mix
  Cooking oil
1 11-ounce can condensed chili beef
  soup *or* one 15½-ounce can chili
  with beans
  Chili powder (optional)
4 ounces sharp Cheddar cheese, sliced
  and cut in wedges

In medium bowl soften yeast in warm water. Add biscuit mix; beat well. Turn out onto cloth dusted with biscuit mix; knead 3 to 5 minutes. Roll dough to a 13-inch circle. Place on a greased 12-inch pizza pan, forming high edges. Brush dough with oil. Bake at 425° for 6 minutes. Spread condensed soup or chili evenly over crust. Sprinkle with chili powder, if desired. Return pizza to oven and bake at 425° for 10 minutes. Top with cheese wedges; bake 5 minutes longer. Makes 4 servings.

Barbecue Beef Pizza

1 15⅜-ounce package cheese
  pizza mix
1 teaspoon prepared mustard
¼ cup chopped onion
1 tablespoon packed brown sugar
1 tablespoon vinegar
1 teaspoon Worcestershire sauce
4 ounces cooked beef, sliced very thin
1 green pepper, cut in rings
½ cup shredded mozzarella cheese
  (2 ounces)

Prepare pizza dough according to package directions. Roll or pat to a 13-inch circle. Place in greased 12-inch pizza pan; crimp edges. Prick with fork; bake at 425° for 8 minutes. In saucepan blend mustard with small amount of pizza sauce from package mix. Add remaining pizza sauce, onion, brown sugar, vinegar, and Worcestershire. Bring to boiling; boil 1 minute. Spread over pizza crust. Cover with beef and pepper rings. Sprinkle with cheese from package mix and mozzarella. Return to oven; bake at 425° about 12 minutes. Serves 4.

Vegetable Garden Pizza

A full-flavored meatless pizza—

1 cup sliced cauliflower
1¼ cups packaged biscuit mix
½ teaspoon dried dillweed
⅓ cup milk
  Cooking oil
  • • •
1 10¾-ounce can cream of potato
  soup
¼ cup milk
1 medium green pepper, cut in strips
1 medium tomato, sliced
2 tablespoons chopped green onion
2 tablespoons snipped parsley
1 cup shredded mozzarella cheese
  (4 ounces)

In saucepan cook cauliflower, covered, in small amount of boiling salted water till tender. Drain and set aside. In mixing bowl combine biscuit mix and dried dillweed. Stir in the ⅓ cup milk. Turn dough out onto a cloth dusted with biscuit mix; knead 8 to 10 strokes. Roll dough into a 13-inch circle. Place on greased 12-inch pizza pan, forming rim around edge. Brush with cooking oil. Bake at 425° for 6 minutes. Combine cream of potato soup and the ¼ cup milk. Spread evenly over the dough. Arrange green pepper strips, tomato slices, and cooked cauliflower atop potato soup. Sprinkle with green onion and parsley. Sprinkle with mozzarella cheese. Return to oven; bake at 425° for 15 to 20 minutes. Makes 4 servings.

Saucy Salami Pizzas

A savory fix-up for frozen cheese pizza—

1 teaspoon dried oregano, crushed
1 8-ounce can tomato sauce
2 12-inch frozen cheese pizzas
4 ounces sliced salami, cut in strips
1 cup shredded Swiss cheese (4 ounces)

Stir oregano into tomato sauce. Spread frozen pizzas with the tomato mixture. Top with strips of salami; sprinkle with Swiss cheese. Place each pizza on a wire rack; set rack on baking sheet. Bake pizzas according to package directions. Makes 4 to 6 servings.

Taco and Tortilla Tempters

Take a tip from our south-of-the-border neighbors and make a tortilla-based snack. In this section you'll find tortillas topped or filled with chicken, beef, a vegetable assortment, shredded cheese, refried beans, ham, ground beef, and shrimp. Each is colorful and tasty.

Chicken Tostadas

Enticing snack shown on pages 4 and 5—

> 8 canned tortillas or frozen
>   tortillas, thawed
> ¼ cup cooking oil
> • • •
> 2 medium chicken breasts, skinned,
>   boned, and cut in very thin
>   strips
> ¼ cup sliced green onion
> 2 tablespoons butter or margarine
> 1 8-ounce can tomato sauce
> ½ teaspoon salt
> ¼ teaspoon garlic salt
> ¼ teaspoon ground cumin
> • • •
> 2 cups shredded lettuce
> 2 medium tomatoes, chopped
> 1 cup shredded Monterey Jack cheese
>   (4 ounces)
> 1 large avocado, seeded, peeled,
>   and sliced
>   Bottled Mexican hot sauce

In small skillet fry tortillas, one at a time, in hot oil till crisp and golden, 30 to 45 seconds on each side. Drain on paper toweling; keep fried tortillas warm in 250° oven. In medium skillet quickly cook chicken strips and sliced green onion in butter or margarine till chicken is browned. Add tomato sauce, salt, garlic salt, and ground cumin. Reduce heat and simmer, covered, 10 to 15 minutes.

To assemble tostadas, place warm tortillas on plate; spoon on chicken mixture. Top with shredded lettuce, chopped tomato, cheese, and avocado slices. Drizzle with bottled Mexican hot sauce to taste. Makes 8 tostadas.

Beef Flautas

> 2 cups cooked beef cut in thin strips
>   (about 12 ounces)
> 1 tablespoon cooking oil
> 1 tablespoon red wine vinegar
> 1½ teaspoons chili powder
> ½ teaspoon dried oregano, crushed
> ½ teaspoon salt
> ⅛ teaspoon garlic powder
>   Cooking oil
> 12 canned tortillas or frozen
>   tortillas, thawed
>   Avocado Sauce

Brown the beef in 1 tablespoon hot oil; drain fat. Add vinegar, chili powder, oregano, salt, and garlic powder, tossing lightly. Set aside. Into a 2-quart saucepan pour oil to depth of 1 inch; heat (do not let smoke). Fry tortillas, one at a time, in oil just till soft and limp but not browned, about 5 seconds. Drain well on paper toweling. Divide beef among tortillas, placing strips at one edge. Starting at filled edge, roll up very tightly. Secure with wooden pick. Fry in the hot oil in saucepan till crisp, about 2 minutes. Lift carefully from oil; drain. Serve with Avocado Sauce. Serves 4 to 6.

Avocado Sauce: Blend together ½ cup mashed ripe avocado (1 medium avocado), 1 teaspoon lemon juice, and ¼ teaspoon salt. Stir in ½ cup dairy sour cream. Stir ½ teaspoon grated lemon peel into avocado mixture.

Vegetable-Tortilla Rolls

Wrap 8 canned tortillas or frozen tortillas, thawed, tightly in foil. Heat in 350° oven till warm, about 10 minutes. Divide 1½ cups shredded Swiss cheese (6 ounces); 1½ cups shredded lettuce; 1 small cucumber, chopped; and one 3-ounce can chopped mushrooms, drained, among the tortillas. Spoon one 7-ounce can frozen avocado dip, thawed, atop tortillas. Sprinkle with bottled Mexican hot sauce. Roll up filled tortillas. Makes 8.

Ham and Bean Tacos

8 taco shells
1 cup diced fully cooked ham
1 tablespoon butter or margarine
½ of a 15-ounce can refried beans
¼ cup dairy sour cream
½ teaspoon chili powder
    Dash garlic powder
        • • •
1 cup shredded Monterey Jack cheese
    (4 ounces)
½ cup shredded lettuce
1 medium tomato, chopped
    Bottled Mexican hot sauce

Warm taco shells according to package directions. Meanwhile, in small skillet brown the ham in butter or margarine. Stir in refried beans, sour cream, chili powder, and garlic powder. Cook over low heat, stirring constantly, till heated through. Spoon ham filling into warm taco shells. Sprinkle cheese and lettuce atop each; top with chopped tomato. Pass bottled Mexican hot sauce. Makes 8 tacos.

Saucy Beef Tacos

12 taco shells
1 pound ground beef
½ cup chopped onion
¾ cup chili sauce *or* bottled
    barbecue sauce
½ teaspoon dried oregano, crushed
½ teaspoon garlic salt
        • • •
2 tomatoes, chopped
2 cups shredded lettuce
1 cup shredded sharp Cheddar cheese
    (4 ounces)
    Bottled Mexican hot sauce

Warm taco shells according to package directions. Meanwhile, in medium skillet cook beef and onion till meat is browned; drain off excess fat. Stir in chili sauce or barbecue sauce, oregano, and garlic salt. Simmer, uncovered, 5 minutes. Spoon about 3 tablespoons meat mixture into each warm taco shell. Top with tomato, lettuce, and shredded cheese. Serve with bottled hot sauce. Makes 12 tacos.

Shrimp-Avocado Tostadas

Begin with avocado dip for a quick topping —

8 canned tortillas or frozen
    tortillas, thawed
¼ cup cooking oil
        • • •
1 7-ounce can frozen avocado dip,
    thawed
¼ cup sliced green onion
1 tablespoon lemon juice
¼ teaspoon garlic salt
2 4½-ounce cans shrimp, drained
        • • •
3 cups shredded lettuce
2 medium tomatoes, chopped
1 cup shredded Cheddar cheese
    (4 ounces)

In small skillet fry tortillas, one at a time, in hot oil till crisp and golden, 30 to 45 seconds on each side. Drain on paper toweling; keep fried tortillas warm in 250° oven. In small bowl combine avocado dip, green onion, lemon juice, and garlic salt; stir in shrimp. To assemble tostadas, spoon some of the shredded lettuce and chopped tomato onto each warm tortilla. Top each with some of the shrimp-avocado mixture. Sprinkle with shredded Cheddar cheese. Makes 8 tostadas.

To assemble *Beef Flautas*, place beef strips at one edge of each tortilla. Roll up tightly, beginning at filled edge, and secure with wooden pick.

Sandwich Bundles

Expand your idea of a sandwich. Instead of spreading the sandwich filling between bread slices, bundle the filling in refrigerated crescent roll dough, bread envelopes, lettuce leaves, or refrigerated biscuit dough. The result is a delicious, fun-to-eat snack.

Reuben Bundles

  1 8-ounce can sauerkraut, drained and
     snipped
 ¼ teaspoon caraway seed
 ½ cup mayonnaise or salad dressing
  2 tablespoons chopped green pepper
  1 tablespoon chopped canned pimiento
  1 tablespoon sliced green onion
  1 tablespoon chili sauce
       • • •
  2 packages refrigerated crescent
     rolls (16 rolls)
     Corned Beef Filling
     Frankfurter Filling
 ½ cup shredded American cheese
     (2 ounces)

Combine snipped sauerkraut and caraway seed; set aside. Combine mayonnaise or salad dressing, green pepper, pimiento, sliced green onion, and chili sauce; mix well. Set aside.

Unroll crescent roll dough; form into eight 6x3½-inch rectangles by pressing perforated edges together. Spoon some of the Corned Beef Filling *or* Frankfurter Filling onto half of each dough rectangle; top with the sauerkraut, mayonnaise mixture, and shredded American cheese. Fold over other half of dough; seal edges with tines of fork. Place on *ungreased* baking sheet. Bake at 425° till golden brown, about 10 minutes. Makes 8 sandwiches.

Corned Beef Filling: In small bowl combine *half* of a 12-ounce can corned beef, chopped (1 cup); ½ cup shredded Swiss cheese; and 1 tablespoon snipped parsley.

Frankfurter Filling: Thinly slice 2 frankfurters. In small bowl combine frankfurters with ¼ cup chopped dill pickle.

Bread Envelopes

 3½ to 4 cups all-purpose flour
  1 package active dry yeast
  2 tablespoons cooking oil
 ¼ teaspoon sugar
     Saucy Beef Filling, scrambled eggs,
      or canned chili with beans, warmed

Advance preparation: In large mixing bowl combine 1¼ *cups* of the flour and the yeast. Combine oil, sugar, 1¼ cups warm water (110°), and 1 teaspoon salt. Add to yeast mixture. Beat at low speed of electric mixer for ½ minute, scraping bowl constantly. Beat 3 minutes at high speed. By hand, stir in enough of the remaining flour to make a moderately stiff dough. Turn out on floured surface; knead till smooth and elastic, about 5 minutes. Place in greased bowl. Cover; let rise about 45 minutes. Punch down; divide in 12 equal parts. Shape in balls. Cover; let rest 10 minutes. Roll each on lightly floured surface to a 5-inch circle, being careful to roll *only* from center outward (*do not roll back and forth*). Place 2 inches apart on *ungreased* baking sheet. Cover; let rise 20 to 30 minutes. Bake at 400° till puffed and lightly browned on bottom, 10 to 12 minutes. Remove; immediately wrap in foil. Cool; freeze.
Before serving: Heat foil-wrapped frozen bread in 350° oven about 10 minutes. Fill with Saucy Beef Filling, eggs, or chili. Makes 12.

Saucy Beef Filling

Quickly cook ½ small green pepper, cut in thin strips, and 2 tablespoons chopped onion in 1 tablespoon cooking oil till crisp-tender. Remove; set aside. Cut 2 beef cube steaks into ¼-inch-wide strips. Brown quickly. Combine ¼ cup cold water, 1 to 2 tablespoons soy sauce, 2 teaspoons cornstarch, ½ teaspoon sugar, and dash ground ginger; add to meat. Cook and stir till bubbly. Stir in pepper, onion, and ½ cup chopped tomato; heat through. Serve in 6 warmed Bread Envelopes. Serves 6.

Whether filled with corned beef and Swiss cheese or a frankfurter mixture, *Reuben Bundles* will draw raves from snackers. Sauerkraut and a dressing mixture complete the hearty filling for these sandwiches.

Cottage Cheesewiches

A unique sandwich featuring a cottage cheese-vegetable filling bundled in a lettuce leaf—

   1 12-ounce carton cream-style cottage cheese (1½ cups)
   ½ cup finely chopped celery
   ¼ cup shredded carrot
   ¼ cup chopped radish
   ¼ teaspoon dried dillweed
   Dash salt
   • • •
   6 lettuce leaves

In mixing bowl mash cottage cheese with fork; stir in chopped celery, shredded carrot, chopped radish, dillweed, and salt. Spread about ⅓ cup cottage cheese mixture on each lettuce leaf. Roll up jelly-roll fashion. Secure with wooden picks. Makes 6 sandwiches.

Pizza-Beef Bundles

Mix ½ pound ground beef; 1 teaspoon dried oregano, crushed; ½ teaspoon salt; and dash pepper. Shape into 5 patties about 3 inches in diameter; brown on both sides. Drain.

Using 1 package refrigerated biscuits (10 biscuits), roll each biscuit to a 4-inch circle on lightly floured surface. Place beef patties atop *half* the dough circles. Using one 3-ounce can chopped mushrooms, drained, and 2 tablespoons chopped onion, spoon some mushrooms and onion onto each patty. Cover with remaining dough circles. Moisten edges; seal with tines of fork. Prick tops of each with fork. Bake on *ungreased* baking sheet at 375° for 8 minutes. Top *each* with a slice of mozzarella cheese; return to oven till cheese melts, 2 to 3 minutes. Heat one 8-ounce can pizza sauce; serve with bundles. Makes 5.

Fruit and Vegetable Nibbles

Have trouble fitting enough fruits and vegetables into your meal plans? Then, use them for snacks. Fresh or canned fruits and vegetables provide necessary vitamins, and they're lower in calories than most other snack foods.

Marinated Fruit Combo

    3 cups cantaloupe and/or honeydew
        melon balls
    1 13¼-ounce can pineapple chunks,
        drained
    1 cup strawberries, hulled
    1 6-ounce can grapefruit juice
    ¼ cup orange marmalade
    2 tablespoons orange liqueur

Advance preparation: Combine melon, pineapple, and strawberries. Combine remaining ingredients; pour over fruits. Stir gently. Chill 1 to 2 hours; stir occasionally. Makes 6 cups.

Pickled Carrots and Zucchini

    ½ cup sugar
    ½ cup vinegar
    1 tablespoon mustard seed
    2 inches stick cinnamon
    3 whole cloves
    3 medium carrots, cut in strips
    1 medium zucchini, cut in strips

Advance preparation: In saucepan mix first 5 ingredients and ½ cup water. Add carrots; cover and simmer till crisp-tender. Add zucchini; return to boiling. Transfer to bowl. Cover; chill at least 8 hours. Makes 3 cups.

Full-flavored marinated snacks

← Be sure to keep *Marinated Fruit Combo* and *Pickled Carrots and Zucchini* on hand for compulsive nibblers. Both snacks are nutritious and good to eat.

Marinated Vegetable Snack
Colorful vegetable mixture shown on the cover —

    2 carrots, cut into sticks
    1 cup broccoli buds
    1 cup cauliflowerets
    1 medium cucumber, sliced
    1 medium zucchini, cut into sticks
    1 small onion, sliced and separated
        into rings
    ½ cup cooking oil
    3 tablespoons white wine vinegar
    1 teaspoon dried oregano, crushed
    ½ teaspoon salt
    ¼ teaspoon pepper

Advance preparation: In saucepan simmer carrots, covered, in small amount of water for 2 minutes. Add broccoli and cauliflower; bring to boiling. Reduce heat; simmer 3 minutes more. Drain. Combine all vegetables. Combine cooking oil, vinegar, oregano, salt, and pepper; pour over vegetables. Cover. Chill at least 8 hours; stir occasionally. Makes 4 cups.

Fix up fruits and vegetables

Fresh and canned fruits and fresh vegetables make tempting snacks by themselves. But don't stop there. Think of other ways to use fruits and vegetables, such as the following:

1. Dip fruit pieces in fruit-flavored yogurt. Then, roll in flaked coconut.

2. Spoon slightly thawed lemonade or orange juice concentrate over fruit.

3. Top fruit such as peaches, plums, or pineapple with a small scoop of sherbet.

4. Fill celery sticks with cheese spread with pimiento or peanut butter.

5. Dip cherry tomatoes, cucumber sticks, celery, carrot sticks, or other vegetables into a purchased sour cream dip.

Basket of Breads

Homemade breads come in a variety of shapes. Form bread dough into long ropes for breadsticks, pull into doughnut shape for bagels, twist and knot dough into soft pretzels, or top with tempting fillings for sweet rolls.

Parmesan Breadsticks

    2 cups all-purpose flour
    ⅓ cup grated Parmesan cheese
    1 package active dry yeast
    ¾ cup milk
    2 tablespoons shortening
    1 tablespoon sugar
    1 teaspoon salt

In large mixing bowl combine *1 cup* of the flour, the Parmesan cheese, and yeast. In saucepan heat milk, shortening, sugar, and salt just till warm (115° to 120°), stirring constantly to melt shortening. Add to dry mixture in mixing bowl. Beat at low speed of electric mixer for ½ minute, scraping bowl constantly. Beat 3 minutes at high speed. By hand, stir in enough remaining flour to make a stiff dough. Shape into a ball. Place in lightly greased bowl, turning once to grease surface.

Cover; let rise in warm place till double, about 1 hour. Punch down; turn out onto floured surface. Divide into 4 portions. Cover; let rest 10 minutes. Divide each portion into 6 pieces. Roll each piece into a pencillike rope 8 inches long. Place on greased baking sheet. Cover; let rise in warm place till double, about 30 minutes. Bake at 375° till golden brown, 10 to 15 minutes. Makes 24 breadsticks.

Sesame Breadsticks

Shape each roll from 1 package refrigerated Parker House rolls (10 rolls) into a pencillike rope 10 inches long. Brush with water; sprinkle with 1 tablespoon sesame seed, toasted. Place on greased baking sheet. Bake at 375° for 9 to 10 minutes. Makes 10 breadsticks.

Crispy Bun Sticks

    3 frankfurter buns, split
    ¼ cup Caesar salad dressing

Cut each bun half lengthwise (to make a total of 12 pieces). Place pieces on baking sheet. Brush each bun stick lightly with salad dressing on all sides, using about *1 teaspoon* for *each* piece. Bake at 375° till lightly browned, 10 to 12 minutes. Makes 12 bun sticks.

Pizza Twists

    1 13¾-ounce package hot roll mix
    1 egg
    1 cup finely chopped pepperoni
      (4 ounces)
    ½ cup shredded Cheddar cheese
      (2 ounces)
    1 tablespoon grated Parmesan cheese
    1 teaspoon instant minced onion
    ½ teaspoon dried oregano, crushed
    ⅛ teaspoon garlic powder
         • • •
    1 beaten egg yolk
    1 tablespoon water

Soften yeast from hot roll mix according to package directions. Stir in 1 egg. Combine flour mixture from the hot roll mix, the pepperoni, cheeses, onion, oregano, and garlic powder. Stir into yeast mixture; mix well. Turn out onto lightly floured surface and knead till smooth. Place in greased bowl, turning once to grease surface. Cover and let rise in warm place till double, about 1 hour. Punch down; turn out onto lightly floured surface. Cut into 24 portions; roll each to a rope 10 inches long. Fold rope in half; twist two or three times. Seal ends with a little water. Place on greased baking sheet. Let rise till almost double, 30 to 45 minutes. Combine egg yolk and water; brush on rolls. Bake at 400° till lightly browned, 12 to 15 minutes. Remove rolls to wire racks to cool. Makes 24 rolls.

Almond-Cherry Circles

2½ cups packaged biscuit mix
⅔ cup milk
¼ teaspoon almond extract
1 to 2 tablespoons butter or
    margarine, softened
¼ cup sugar
1 teaspoon ground cinnamon
¾ cup cherry preserves

Combine biscuit mix, milk, and almond extract. Turn out onto floured surface; knead gently 8 to 10 strokes. Roll dough to 12x7-inch rectangle. Spread with butter. Mix sugar and cinnamon; sprinkle over dough. Roll up, starting with long side; seal seam. Cut into 1-inch slices. Place on greased baking sheet. Flatten slightly with palm of hand. Make large depression in center with fingers. Bake at 375° for 12 to 15 minutes. Spoon 1 tablespoon preserves into center of each. Makes 12 rolls.

Black Bottom Twirls

¼ cup butter or margarine, melted
½ cup chocolate-caramel topping
1 tablespoon milk
⅓ cup chopped pecans
2 packages refrigerated crescent
    rolls (16 rolls)
Ground cinnamon

Divide butter among 12 muffin pans. Combine topping and milk; spoon about *1 teaspoon* topping mixture into *each* pan. Sprinkle with pecans. Unroll crescent rolls to form 8 rectangles; press perforations to seal. Spread rectangles with remaining topping mixture; sprinkle lightly with cinnamon. Roll up, starting with short side. Slice each into 3 rolls. Place 2 rolls, cut side down, in each muffin pan. Bake at 375° for 20 to 25 minutes. Loosen sides and invert. Spoon any glaze remaining in pan over rolls. Makes 12 rolls.

Bake an assortment of breads for your family or friends to sample. Be sure to include peppy *Pizza Twists; Light Rye Bagels,* a variation of *Bagels* (see recipe, page 25); and golden, cheese-flecked *Parmesan Breadsticks.*

Italian Herb Breadsticks

In mixing bowl soften the yeast from one 13¾-ounce package hot roll mix in ½ cup warm water (110°). Add flour mixture from roll mix, ½ cup dairy sour cream, 1 egg, 1 teaspoon fennel seed, and ½ teaspoon dried oregano, crushed. Mix well. Turn out on floured surface; knead 1 minute. Place in greased bowl; turn once. Cover; let rise in warm place till double, 50 to 60 minutes. Punch down; turn out on floured surface. Cover; let rest 10 minutes. Divide into six portions. Divide each portion into 8 pieces. Roll each piece to form a pencillike rope 12 inches long. Place on greased baking sheets. Brush with water; sprinkle lightly with coarse salt. Let rise till almost double, 20 to 30 minutes. Bake at 400° till golden brown, 10 to 12 minutes. Makes 48.

To make *Soft Whole Wheat Pretzels,* first form a knot, then loop ends through. Before baking, sprinkle these snacks lightly with coarse salt.

Raspberry Fantans

Combine ¼ cup raspberry preserves, ½ teaspoon grated lemon peel, and ¼ teaspoon ground cinnamon. Separate each roll from 1 package refrigerated butterflake rolls into 3 sections. Spread about ½ *teaspoon* preserve mixture on 2 sections of *each* roll; reassemble. Place on edge in greased 2-inch muffin pans. Bake at 375° for 12 to 14 minutes. Makes 12.

Soft Whole Wheat Pretzels

   3 cups all-purpose flour
1½ tablespoons sesame seed, toasted
   1 package active dry yeast
2½ cups milk
   ½ cup sugar
   ¼ cup cooking oil
   3 cups whole wheat flour
   1 slightly beaten egg white
     Coarse salt *or* sesame seed, toasted

In mixing bowl combine *2 cups* of the all-purpose flour, the 1½ tablespoons sesame seed, and yeast. Heat milk, sugar, oil, and 1½ teaspoons salt just till warm (115° to 120°). Add to dry mixture. Beat at low speed of electric mixer for ½ minute, scraping bowl. Beat 3 minutes at high speed. By hand, stir in whole wheat flour and enough remaining all-purpose flour to make a moderately stiff dough. Knead on floured surface till smooth, about 5 minutes. Shape into a ball. Place in greased bowl; turn once. Cover; let rise till double, about 50 minutes. Punch down; turn out on floured surface. Cover; let rest 10 minutes.

Roll to a 12x12-inch square. Cut into strips 12 inches long and ½ inch wide. Roll each to a rope 16 inches long. Shape into pretzels by forming a knot and looping ends through. Let rise, uncovered, 20 minutes. Dissolve 3 tablespoons salt in 2 quarts boiling water. Lower 1 or 2 pretzels at a time into boiling water; boil for 1 minute on each side. Remove to paper toweling with slotted spoon; pat dry. Arrange ½ inch apart on well-greased baking sheets. Brush with mixture of egg white and 1 tablespoon water. Sprinkle lightly with coarse salt or sesame seed. Bake at 350° till golden brown, about 25 minutes. Makes 24 pretzels.

Bagels

A variation, Light Rye Bagels, shown on page 23 —

4¼ to 4½ cups all-purpose flour
2 packages active dry yeast
1½ cups warm water (110°)
3 tablespoons sugar
1 tablespoon salt
1 gallon water
1 tablespoon sugar

In large mixing bowl combine *1½ cups* of the all-purpose flour and the yeast. Combine the 1½ cups warm water, 3 tablespoons sugar, and salt. Add to dry mixture in mixing bowl. Beat at low speed of electric mixer for ½ minute, scraping sides of bowl constantly. Beat 3 minutes at high speed. By hand, stir in enough of the remaining flour to make a moderately stiff dough. Turn out onto lightly floured surface and knead till smooth and elastic, 8 to 10 minutes. Cover and let rest 15 minutes.

Cut into 12 portions. Shape into smooth balls. Punch a hole in center of each with a floured finger. Pull gently to form a 1½-inch hole, working each bagel into uniform shape. Cover and let rise 20 minutes. (Optional step for glossy, smooth surface: Place raised bagels on *ungreased* baking sheet and broil 4 to 5 inches from heat for 1½ to 2 minutes.)

In large kettle combine 1 gallon water and 1 tablespoon sugar; bring to boiling. Reduce heat to simmering; cook 4 or 5 bagels at a time for 7 minutes, turning once. Drain. Place on well-greased baking sheet. Bake at 375° about 30 minutes. (For bagels that have been broiled, bake 20 to 25 minutes.) Remove from baking sheet; cool on wire rack. Makes 12 bagels.

Garlic Bagels: Prepare Bagels as above, *except* combine 1 teaspoon garlic powder with the all-purpose flour and yeast mixture.

Light Rye Bagels: Prepare Bagels as above, *except* use 3¼ to 3½ cups all-purpose flour and 1¼ cups rye flour. Combine *1½ cups* of the all-purpose flour and the yeast; add 1½ teaspoons caraway seed. Continue to combine warm water, sugar, and salt and beat, as directed. Then by hand, stir in the rye flour and enough of the remaining all-purpose flour to make a moderately stiff dough.

For chewy bagels, boil the raised dough in sugared water for a few minutes before baking. Use tongs to turn and remove bagels, then pat dry with towels.

Oatmeal Pretzels

3 cups all-purpose flour
1 package active dry yeast
2 tablespoons cooking oil
1 tablespoon sugar
1¼ cups quick-cooking rolled oats

In mixing bowl combine *1½ cups* of the flour and the yeast. Combine oil, sugar, 1½ cups warm water (110°), and 1½ teaspoons salt. Add to dry mixture. Beat at low speed of electric mixer for ½ minute, scraping bowl. Beat 3 minutes at high speed. By hand, stir in oats and remaining flour to make a moderately stiff dough. Knead on floured surface till smooth. Place in greased bowl; turn once. Cover; let rise till double, about 40 minutes. Punch down; cover and let rest 10 minutes. Cut into 16 portions; let rest 10 minutes longer. Roll each to a rope 16 inches long. Shape into pretzels by forming a knot and looping ends through. Let rise, uncovered, till almost double, about 25 minutes. Dissolve 3 tablespoons salt in 2 quarts boiling water. Lower 1 or 2 pretzels at a time into boiling water; boil for 1 minute on each side. Remove; pat dry. Arrange ½ inch apart on greased baking sheets. Bake at 350° for 20 to 25 minutes. Brush with 1 tablespoon melted butter, if desired. Makes 16.

Dessert Dramatics

The next time you have the urge for a sweet snack, fix a special dessert. You'll have fun preparing and eating decorative cookies, candies, luscious sundaes, frozen sicles, and fresh-tasting ice creams and sherbets.

Red Lollipops

    3 cups sugar
    ¾ cup light corn syrup
    ⅓ cup boiling water
    3 tablespoons vinegar
      Several drops red food coloring
    ¼ cup butter or margarine
      Fruit-flavored hard candy circles

Combine first 5 ingredients; stir till sugar dissolves. Cook till hard-crack stage (300° on candy thermometer). Remove from heat; stir in butter and dash salt. Cool till slightly thick. Place 15 wooden skewers 5 inches apart on greased baking sheets. Quickly drop sugar mixture from tablespoon over skewers to form lollipops 3 inches in diameter. Make faces with candy circles. Makes 15 lollipops.

Candied Orange Peel

    6 medium oranges
    2 cups sugar
      Sugar

Advance preparation: Cut peel of each orange in sixths; loosen from pulp. Remove most of white membrane from peel. Add peel and 1 tablespoon salt to 4 cups water. Place a plate over top to keep peel under water. Let stand overnight. Drain; wash. Place peel in saucepan. Cover with cold water. Heat to boiling; drain. Repeat boiling and draining 3 times. With kitchen shears, cut peel in strips. Combine peel, 2 cups sugar, and ½ cup water. Heat and stir till sugar dissolves. Cook slowly till peel is translucent. Drain; roll in additional sugar. Dry on rack overnight. Makes 2 cups.

Molasses Taffy

    1½ cups sugar
     1 cup light molasses
     ½ cup light corn syrup
     ¼ teaspoon baking soda
     2 tablespoons butter or margarine
     ½ cup chopped walnuts

Combine sugar, molasses, corn syrup, and ¼ cup water. Stir to dissolve sugar. Cook and stir over medium-low heat for 15 to 20 minutes. Raise temperature to medium; cook, stirring often, till hard-ball stage (265° on candy thermometer), 40 to 45 minutes. Add soda; stir in butter. Stir in nuts. Pour into greased shallow pan. When cool enough to handle, pull till opaque and lighter in color. Form into ropes. With kitchen shears, cut into 1-inch pieces. Wrap in clear plastic wrap. Makes 72.

Candy Cane Popcorn Balls

    20 cups popped corn
     2 cups sugar
     ½ cup light corn syrup
     1 teaspoon vinegar
     1 teaspoon vanilla
    15 to 20 candy canes

Keep popped corn warm in 225° oven. Butter sides of saucepan. Combine sugar, syrup, vinegar, 1½ cups water, and ½ teaspoon salt. Cook till hard-ball stage (250° on candy thermometer). Stir in vanilla. Slowly pour over corn; stir just to mix well. Butter hands; shape mixture into balls around candy. Makes 15 to 20.

Festive cookies and candies

Enjoy *Red Lollipops, Candy Cane Popcorn Balls,* → *Gingerbread Men, Orange Fondant-Stuffed Dates, Spritz Cookies, Molasses Taffy, Candied Orange Peel,* or *Cherry-Almond Cookies* at snack time. (See index for recipe page numbers.)

Chocolate-Covered Cherries

Purchase dipping chocolate at a candy store or a large supermarket —

60 maraschino cherries with stems
3 tablespoons butter or margarine
3 tablespoons light corn syrup
¼ teaspoon salt
2 cups sifted powdered sugar
1½ pounds dipping chocolate

Advance preparation: Drain cherries well; let stand on paper toweling. Combine butter or margarine, corn syrup, and salt; stir in powdered sugar to make fondant. Knead till smooth. Chill. Shape about 1 teaspoon fondant mixture around each cherry. Place on baking sheet lined with waxed paper; chill.

In small, heavy saucepan or deep bowl over pan of hot water, melt dipping chocolate, stirring constantly. *Do not add any liquid.* Holding onto stems, dip fondant-covered cherries, one at a time, into melted chocolate. Spoon chocolate over cherries to coat. Place on baking sheet lined with waxed paper. Chill till chocolate hardens. Store in covered container in cool place. Let ripen a week or two so fondant will begin to liquefy. Makes 60.

Apple-Peanut Butter Fudge

1 6-ounce package semisweet chocolate pieces (1 cup)
½ of a 7-, 9-, or 10-ounce jar marshmallow creme (about 1 cup)
½ cup peanut butter
1 teaspoon vanilla
2 cups sugar
⅔ cup apple juice

Combine chocolate, marshmallow creme, peanut butter, and vanilla; set aside. Butter sides of heavy 2-quart saucepan. Combine sugar and apple juice. Cook and stir over medium heat till sugar dissolves and mixture boils. Cook till soft-ball stage (240° on candy thermometer), stirring often. Remove from heat; quickly add the chocolate mixture. Stir just till blended. Pour into buttered 9x9x2-inch pan. Top with chopped peanuts, if desired. Cut when firm. Makes about 40 pieces.

Gingerbread Men

A cookie favorite pictured on page 27 —

1½ cups sugar
1 cup butter or margarine
1 egg
2 tablespoons dark corn syrup
4 teaspoons grated orange peel
3 cups all-purpose flour
2 teaspoons baking soda
2 teaspoons ground cinnamon
1 teaspoon ground ginger
½ teaspoon ground cloves
½ teaspoon salt

Advance preparation: Thoroughly cream together sugar and butter. Add egg; beat till light and fluffy. Add corn syrup and orange peel; mix well. Stir flour, soda, cinnamon, ginger, cloves, and salt together thoroughly; stir into creamed mixture. Chill dough thoroughly.
Before serving: On lightly floured surface roll dough ¼ inch thick. Cut with gingerbread man cookie cutter. Place 1 inch apart on *ungreased* cookie sheet. Bake at 375° for 8 to 10 minutes. Cool 1 minute; remove from sheet. Cool on wire rack. Decorate as desired. Makes 24.

Cherry-Almond Cookies

Cherry-studded cookies pictured on page 27 —

½ cup butter or margarine
½ cup sugar
1 egg yolk
1 tablespoon milk
¼ teaspoon salt
¼ teaspoon almond extract
1¼ cups all-purpose flour
1 slightly beaten egg white
1 cup chopped blanched almonds
Red and green maraschino cherries

Advance preparation: Thoroughly cream together butter and sugar. Add egg yolk, milk, salt, and extract; beat well. Stir in flour. Chill.
Before serving: Form dough into 1-inch balls. Dip in beaten egg white; roll in chopped almonds. Place on greased cookie sheet; flatten slightly. Halve cherries; press cherry half in center of each cookie. Bake at 325° for 20 to 25 minutes. Makes about 24 cookies.

Finnish Chestnut Fingers

    6 tablespoons butter or margarine
    ¼ cup sugar
    1 egg yolk
    ½ cup chestnut purée *or* canned
        chestnuts, drained and pureed
    ¼ teaspoon vanilla
    1 cup all-purpose flour
    ¼ teaspoon salt
    ¼ teaspoon ground cinnamon
    1 slightly beaten egg white
        Sugar
    ½ cup semisweet chocolate pieces,
        melted

Cream butter or margarine and the ¼ cup sugar thoroughly. Add egg yolk; beat till light and fluffy. Beat in chestnut purée and vanilla. Stir flour, salt, and cinnamon together thoroughly; stir into creamed mixture. Roll into 2½-inch-long fingers, using a scant tablespoon dough for each finger. Dip one side of each finger in slightly beaten egg white, then in sugar. Place, sugar side up, on greased cookie sheet. Bake at 350° till lightly browned, about 20 minutes. Remove from cookie sheet while hot. Cool on wire rack. Dip one end of each cookie in melted chocolate. Place on waxed paper till chocolate hardens. Makes 30 cookies.

Spritz Cookies

Decorative cookies shown on page 27—

    1½ cups butter or margarine
    1 cup sugar
    1 egg
    1 tablespoon milk
    1 teaspoon vanilla
    ½ teaspoon almond extract
    4 cups all-purpose flour
    1 teaspoon baking powder

Thoroughly cream together butter and sugar. Add egg, milk, vanilla, and almond extract; beat well. Stir flour and baking powder together thoroughly. Gradually add to creamed mixture, mixing till smooth. Force dough through cookie press onto *ungreased* cookie sheet. Decorate as desired. Bake at 400° for 8 to 10 minutes. Makes 48 cookies.

Orange Fondant-Stuffed Dates

Candy and fruit snack shown on page 27—

    1½ cups sifted powdered sugar
    2 tablespoons butter or margarine
    ¼ teaspoon grated orange peel
    4 teaspoons orange juice
    ¼ teaspoon orange extract
    1 8-ounce package pitted dates

Cream together powdered sugar and butter. Mix in orange peel, juice, and extract. Place in pastry tube; pipe into dates. Makes about 32.

English Toffee Ice Cream

    4 1⅛-ounce chocolate-coated English
        toffee bars
    2 cups whipping cream
    1 14-ounce can *sweetened condensed
        milk*
    ½ cup strong coffee, cooled
    1½ teaspoons vanilla

Advance preparation: Place toffee bars between two pieces of waxed paper; crush with rolling pin. Set aside. Combine remaining ingredients; chill well. Whip to custardlike consistency. Fold in crushed toffee. Spoon cream mixture into three 3-cup refrigerator trays. Freeze firm. Makes 8 cups ice cream.

Maple-Almond Ice Cream

    3 egg yolks
    ¾ cup maple-flavored syrup
    1 5⅓-ounce can evaporated milk,
        chilled icy cold (⅔ cup)
    3 egg whites
    ¼ teaspoon cream of tartar
    ½ cup chopped almonds, toasted

Advance preparation: Beat egg yolks well; stir in syrup. Cook and stir over low heat till mixture thickens. Cool well. Whip evaporated milk to soft peaks; fold into syrup mixture. Beat egg whites and cream of tartar till stiff peaks form. Fold into syrup mixture along with almonds. Pour into two 3-cup refrigerator trays; freeze firm. Makes 6 cups.

Fruit Juice Sherbet

1 cup mashed fully ripe banana
  (2 medium bananas)
⅔ cup sugar
½ teaspoon grated orange peel
⅓ cup orange juice
1 tablespoon lemon juice
• • •
1 cup cranberry juice cocktail
6 drops red food coloring
1 stiffly beaten egg white

Advance preparation: Combine mashed banana, sugar, orange peel, orange juice, and lemon juice. Beat till smooth. Stir in cranberry juice cocktail and red food coloring. Turn into 4-cup refrigerator tray; freeze firm. Break mixture into chunks; turn into chilled mixing bowl. Using chilled beaters, beat mixture with electric mixer or rotary beater till smooth. Fold in egg white; return to cold refrigerator tray. Freeze till cranberry mixture is firm.
Before serving: Let stand at room temperature for a few minutes. Makes 4 cups sherbet.

Lemon-Nut Sherbet

Ice cream fans of all ages will enjoy this tangy, walnut-filled sherbet—

2 eggs
½ cup sugar
• • •
2 cups light cream
½ cup light corn syrup
2 teaspoons grated lemon peel
¼ cup lemon juice
½ cup chopped walnuts

Advance preparation: Beat eggs till thick and lemon-colored. Add the sugar gradually; beat till thick. Stir in light cream, light corn syrup, grated lemon peel, and lemon juice. Pour cream mixture into two 3-cup refrigerator trays; freeze till firm, about 2½ hours. Break mixture into chunks; turn into chilled mixing bowl. Using chilled beaters, beat mixture with electric mixer or rotary beater till smooth. Stir in chopped walnuts. Return mixture quickly to cold refrigerator trays and freeze till mixture is firm. Makes 5 cups sherbet.

Apricot Mousse

1 17-ounce can unpeeled apricot
  halves, drained and mashed
½ cup sifted powdered sugar
½ teaspoon vanilla
¼ teaspoon almond extract
1 cup whipping cream

Advance preparation: Combine apricots, sugar, vanilla, extract, and dash salt. Whip cream till custardlike; fold into apricot mixture. Turn into a 3-cup refrigerator tray; freeze till firm, about 4 hours. Makes about 3 cups.

Upside-Down Sundaes

6 balls vanilla ice cream
1 cup chopped peanuts
1 3¾- or 4-ounce package *regular*
  butterscotch pudding mix
⅔ cup dark corn syrup
⅓ cup chunk-style peanut butter
1¾ cups milk

Roll ice cream balls in peanuts to coat; freeze till firm. Meanwhile, combine pudding mix, corn syrup, and peanut butter. Gradually stir in milk. Cook, stirring constantly, till thickened and bubbly. Cook 2 minutes longer. Pour a generous amount of pudding mixture into individual dessert dishes. Set peanut-covered ice cream ball atop. If desired, garnish with frozen whipped dessert topping, thawed. Serves 6.

Tropical Fruit Sundaes

1 small ripe banana, mashed
2 teaspoons lemon juice
½ cup orange marmalade
½ cup apricot-pineapple preserves
½ teaspoon rum flavoring
  Vanilla ice cream
  Flaked coconut, toasted

Combine banana and lemon juice; stir in marmalade and preserves. Cook, stirring constantly, till heated through. Remove from heat; stir in rum flavoring. Spoon over ice cream. Sprinkle with coconut. Makes 1½ cups sauce.

Cherry-Creme Cones

    1 21-ounce can cherry pie filling
    1 7-, 9-, or 10-ounce jar marshmallow
        creme
    10 drops almond extract
    1 cup whipping cream
    10 ice cream cones

Advance preparation: Combine pie filling, marshmallow creme, and almond extract. Whip cream; fold into cherry mixture. Turn into a 9x5x3-inch loaf pan. Cover; freeze firm.
Before serving: Scoop into cones. Makes 10.

Orange Eggnog Sicles

    1 pint vanilla ice cream
    1 6-ounce can frozen orange juice
        concentrate, thawed
    1 egg
    1½ cups milk
    12 wooden sticks

Advance preparation: Beat together ice cream, concentrate, and egg with electric mixer. Gradually add milk, beating constantly. Pour about ⅓ cup mixture into each of twelve 3-ounce waxed-paper drink cups. Place in freezer. When partially frozen, insert wooden sticks. Freeze till mixture is firm.
Before serving: Peel off paper. Makes 12.

Pineapple-Blueberry Sicles

    1 8¼-ounce can crushed pineapple
    1 8-ounce carton blueberry yogurt
    1 6-ounce can frozen pineapple juice
        concentrate, thawed
    1 juice can water (⅔ cup)
    ⅓ cup sugar
    10 wooden sticks

Advance preparation: Combine undrained pineapple and blueberry yogurt. Stir in concentrate, water, and sugar. Pour about ⅓ cup mixture into each of ten 3-ounce waxed-paper drink cups. Place in freezer. When partially frozen, insert wooden sticks. Freeze firm.
Before serving: Peel off paper. Makes 10.

Personality Pudding Tarts

    1 5-ounce can chocolate pudding
    1 5-ounce can vanilla pudding
    1 5-ounce can lemon pudding
    1 5-ounce can butterscotch pudding
    20 Tiny Tart Shells *or* purchased
        tart shells
        Assorted toppings: whipped cream
        or whipped dessert topping, fruit,
        semisweet chocolate pieces,
        toasted nuts, coconut, chocolate
        syrup, and/or tiny candies

Spoon chocolate, vanilla, lemon, and butterscotch pudding into Tiny Tart Shells or purchased tart shells, using about one tablespoon in each. Top with one or more of the assorted toppings as desired. Makes 20 tarts.

Tiny Tart Shells: In mixing bowl combine 2 sticks piecrust mix and ¼ cup sugar. Stir and toss in ¼ cup hot water till dough holds together. Using about 1 tablespoon dough for each, press into 2-inch tart pans to make 20 tart shells. Bake at 450° till golden brown, 8 to 10 minutes. Cool tart shells slightly before removing from pans.

Be creative when decorating *Personality Pudding Tarts*. Use assorted fresh and canned fruits, nuts, candies, chocolate pieces, and other toppings.

All-Occasion Snacks

Whatever the occasion, snacks and good times go hand-in-hand—especially when the snacks are as delicious and easy to make as the ones in this section.

When the occasion calls for a snack to nibble on, take your pick from an assortment of cereal mixes, flavored popcorn, nut snacks, and cheese wafers. Dig into a sandwich when you want a hearty snack. For a sweet snack, select a candy, cookie, or caramel apple. You'll also find hot and cold dips, cheese spreads, popcorn balls, milk shakes, thick malts, parfaits, sauces for sundaes, and other popular snacks.

And if you're counting calories, select one of the many tasty low-calorie recipes. Simply follow the suggestions for fitting these calorie-trimmed snacks and beverages in your diet.

You'll enjoy snacking on *Frosty Dipped Bananas, Molasses Popcorn, Peach Parfaits, Double Raspberry Fizzers, Purple Cows, Frozen Chocolate Sticks, Marshmallow Squares,* and *Homemade Gumdrops.* (See index for recipe page numbers.)

Dips and Spreads

Hot Broccoli Dip

2 10-ounce packages frozen chopped broccoli
2 cups dairy sour cream
2 envelopes beef-flavored mushroom soup mix
2 teaspoons Worcestershire sauce
2 cloves garlic, crushed
Assorted crackers

Cook broccoli according to package directions; drain, reserving liquid. Add water to liquid to make 1 cup. Place broccoli, broccoli liquid, and sour cream in blender container. Cover; blend till smooth, stopping to scrape down sides once or twice. Pour into saucepan. Add soup mix, Worcestershire, and garlic; heat through. Transfer to fondue pot; place over fondue burner. If desired, garnish with parsley and lemon. Serve with crackers. Makes 4 cups.

Blue Cheese Pâté

2 slices bacon
1 8-ounce package cream cheese, softened
1 4¾-ounce can liver spread
½ cup crumbled blue cheese (2 ounces)
2 tablespoons dry sherry
½ of an 8-ounce can water chestnuts, drained and chopped (½ cup)
2 tablespoons minced onion
2 tablespoons chopped pimiento-stuffed green olives
Raw vegetables (see tip, page 36)

Advance preparation: Cook bacon till crisp; drain. Crumble; set aside. In small mixing bowl beat together cream cheese, liver spread, blue cheese, and sherry till fluffy. Stir in water chestnuts, onion, olives, and bacon. Turn into small bowl or mold; chill till firm.
Before serving: Unmold. Garnish with sieved hard-cooked egg yolk, if desired. Serve with raw vegetables. Makes about 2⅔ cups spread.

Green Goddess Dip

¾ cup mayonnaise or salad dressing
¾ cup dairy sour cream
¼ cup snipped parsley
2 tablespoons snipped chives
1 tablespoon anchovy paste
1 teaspoon lemon juice
1 small clove garlic, crushed
Vegetable dippers (see tip, page 36)

Advance preparation: Combine mayonnaise, sour cream, parsley, chives, anchovy paste, lemon juice, and garlic. Chill till ready to serve.
Before serving: Garnish dip with additional snipped chives, if desired. Serve with crisp vegetable dippers. Makes 1½ cups dip.

Creamy Curry Dip

Chutney accents the curry and adds sweetness—

¼ cup tomato sauce
1 teaspoon instant minced onion
1 teaspoon Worcestershire sauce
½ teaspoon curry powder
1 8-ounce package Neufchâtel cheese, softened
3 tablespoons chutney
Assorted crackers

In small mixing bowl combine tomato sauce, instant minced onion, Worcestershire sauce, and curry powder; let mixture stand 10 minutes. Add softened Neufchâtel cheese. Beat at medium speed of electric mixer till cheese mixture is creamy. Turn into serving bowl. Garnish dip with a ring of chutney. Serve with assorted crackers. Makes about 1 cup dip.

Colorful dips and dippers

Serve fresh, crisp vegetables and assorted crackers →
with *Blue Cheese Pâté, Hot Broccoli Dip,* chutney-ringed *Creamy Curry Dip,* and *Green Goddess Dip.*

Pineapple-Orange Yogurt Dip

1 8¼-ounce can crushed pineapple, chilled
1 8-ounce carton orange yogurt
1 4-ounce container whipped cream cheese
¼ cup flaked coconut, toasted
2 tablespoons packed brown sugar
  Milk
  Fruit dippers

Drain pineapple well. Combine pineapple, yogurt, cream cheese, toasted coconut, and brown sugar. If necessary, add milk for dipping consistency. Chill till serving time. Garnish dip with orange slices, if desired. Serve with assorted fruit dippers. Makes 2 cups dip.

Cheese Snack Spread

1 cup shredded sharp Cheddar cheese
1 hard-cooked egg, chopped
¼ cup minced dill pickle
2 tablespoons minced green pepper
1 tablespoon minced onion
1 tablespoon chopped canned pimiento
2 tablespoons mayonnaise
  Assorted crackers

Combine cheese, egg, dill pickle, green pepper, onion, and pimiento; stir in mayonnaise. Chill till serving time. Serve with crackers or as a sandwich spread. Makes 1¼ cups spread.

Braunschweiger Dip

½ pound braunschweiger
1 cup dairy sour cream
2 tablespoons onion soup mix
1 tablespoon milk
1 teaspoon Worcestershire sauce
  Few drops bottled hot pepper sauce
  Vegetable dippers or crackers

In small mixing bowl combine braunschweiger, sour cream, onion soup mix, milk, Worcestershire, and hot pepper sauce. Beat till blended. Chill till ready to serve. Serve with vegetable dippers or crackers. Makes about 2 cups dip.

Cucumber and Bacon Dip

4 slices bacon
2 cups dairy sour cream
½ cup grated cucumber
1 envelope onion salad dressing mix
2 tablespoons chopped canned pimiento
2 tablespoons lemon juice
½ teaspoon Worcestershire sauce
  Vegetable dippers

Advance preparation: Cook bacon till crisp; drain. Crumble; set aside. Mix sour cream, cucumber, dressing mix, pimiento, juice, and Worcestershire. Chill at least ½ hour.
Before serving: Stir in crumbled bacon. Serve with vegetable dippers. Makes about 2 cups.

Italian-Seasoned Gouda Spread

Bring one 8-ounce Gouda *or* Edam cheese to room temperature; cut circle from top. Hollow out, leaving ¼ inch cheese on all sides. Cut up cheese. Combine cut-up cheese, ½ cup dairy sour cream, and 1½ teaspoons Italian salad dressing mix. Beat smooth. Spoon into shell. Chill till ready to serve. Serve with crackers or apple wedges. Makes about 1¼ cups.

Dipper suggestions

Add interest and appeal to dips and spreads by serving a varied assortment of dippers. Crisp, cold, raw vegetables such as carrots, celery, green pepper, cucumber, zucchini, cherry tomatoes, cauliflowerets, mushrooms, and radishes are colorful and fresh tasting. For fruit dips, select strawberries, seedless grapes, cherries, apples, pears, and pineapple. Brush cut fruits with lemon juice to prevent browning. Also, cooked meat cubes and shrimp go well with many dips.

Offer a selection of crackers and chips in many flavors and shapes. To recrisp crackers, spread on a baking sheet and heat at 350° for 3 to 5 minutes.

Creamy Vegetable Dip

1 8-ounce package cream cheese,
    softened
⅓ cup mayonnaise or salad dressing
1 tablespoon anchovy paste
1 hard-cooked egg, finely chopped
¼ cup snipped parsley
2 tablespoons finely chopped onion
1 small clove garlic, minced
    Vegetable dippers

Blend together cream cheese, mayonnaise, and anchovy paste. Stir in chopped egg, parsley, onion, and garlic. Chill till serving time. Serve with vegetables. Makes 1¾ cups dip.

Frankfurter Pâté

½ pound frankfurters, sliced (4 or 5)
2 3-ounce packages cream
    cheese, softened
1 thin slice onion
4 teaspoons milk
1 tablespoon chili sauce
2 teaspoons lemon juice
2 teaspoons Worcestershire sauce
    Dash bottled hot pepper sauce
1 hard-cooked egg, sieved
    Assorted crackers

Advance preparation: Place first 8 ingredients in blender container. Cover and blend smooth, stopping to scrape sides often. Chill mixture in small mold or bowl till firm.
Before serving: Unmold. Garnish with sieved egg. Serve with crackers. Makes 1⅔ cups.

Cream Cheese-Chili Dip

In saucepan combine one 11-ounce can condensed chili beef soup and one 3-ounce package cream cheese, softened. Heat slowly, stirring constantly, till blended. Stir in ½ cup dairy sour cream, 1 teaspoon prepared mustard, and ½ teaspoon Worcestershire sauce. Heat through. Stir in 1 tablespoon water. Transfer to fondue pot or small chafing dish. Keep warm over fondue or chafing dish burner. Serve with tortilla chips or corn chips. Makes about 2 cups.

Hot Bean and Cheese Dip

1 11½-ounce can condensed
    bean with bacon soup
1 cup shredded sharp American cheese
¼ cup finely chopped canned green
    chili peppers
1 teaspoon instant minced onion
    Dash garlic powder
    Corn chips or tortilla chips

In saucepan combine first 5 ingredients and ¼ cup water. Heat slowly, stirring constantly, till heated through. Transfer to fondue pot or small chafing dish. Keep warm over fondue or chafing dish burner. Add water to thin, as necessary. Serve with chips. Makes about 2 cups.

Peppy Cheese Dip

1 cup small curd cream-style cottage
    cheese
1 5-ounce jar process cheese spread
    with pimiento
1 teaspoon prepared horseradish
2 drops bottled hot pepper sauce
    Vegetable dippers

Combine all ingredients *except* vegetables; beat well. Chill till serving time. Serve with vegetables. Makes about 1½ cups dip.

Baked Shrimp Spread

1 8-ounce package cream cheese,
    softened
2 tablespoons dry sherry
1 4½-ounce can shrimp, drained and
    chopped
1 tablespoon snipped chives
¼ teaspoon prepared horseradish
½ cup dairy sour cream
    Paprika
    Unsalted crackers or melba toast

Blend cheese and sherry; stir in shrimp, chives, and horseradish. Stir in sour cream. Spread in 8-inch pie plate or flan pan. Sprinkle with paprika. Bake at 350° for 25 to 30 minutes. Spread hot mixture on crackers. Makes 2 cups.

Deviled Ham and Cheese Ball

2 3-ounce packages cream
   cheese, softened
1 4½-ounce can deviled ham
1 tablespoon snipped chives
1 teaspoon prepared mustard
¼ cup coarsely chopped macadamia nuts
   Assorted crackers

Advance preparation: Blend together cream cheese, deviled ham, chives, and mustard. Line a 2-cup mold or bowl with clear plastic wrap or foil. Press cheese mixture into bowl; chill till firm, 3 to 4 hours or overnight.
Before serving: Unmold. Smooth with a small spatula. Garnish with nuts. Sprinkle lightly with additional snipped chives, if desired. Let stand 10 minutes before serving. Serve with crackers. Makes about 1½ cups.

Hot Bean Dunk

1 cup cream-style cottage cheese
1 15½-ounce can red kidney beans,
   drained and rinsed
1 envelope chili seasoning mix
   Corn chips

In blender container blend cottage cheese at low speed till smooth. Add kidney beans and chili seasoning mix. Cover and blend at low speed till combined, stopping blender to scrape down sides once or twice. Blend at high speed till mixture is nearly smooth, a few seconds more. Serve with corn chips. Makes 2 cups dip.

Lickety Split Dip

1 cup dairy sour cream
½ cup American cheese spread
¼ cup chili sauce
2 tablespoons vegetable soup mix
½ teaspoon Worcestershire sauce
   Vegetable dippers (see tip, page 36)

Combine sour cream, cheese spread, chili sauce, vegetable soup mix, and Worcestershire. Beat till smooth. Chill till ready to serve. Serve with vegetable dippers. Makes 2 cups dip.

Curry-Sour Cream Dip

1 cup dairy sour cream
1 cup mayonnaise or salad dressing
2 teaspoons curry powder
½ teaspoon grated onion
½ teaspoon prepared horseradish
   Dash garlic powder
   Vegetable dippers (see tip, page 36)

Combine sour cream, mayonnaise or salad dressing, curry powder, grated onion, horseradish, and garlic powder; chill till ready to serve. Serve with vegetables. Makes 2 cups.

Chutney and Cheese Spread

4 3-ounce packages cream
   cheese, softened
2 cups shredded sharp Cheddar
   cheese (8 ounces)
2 tablespoons dry sherry
1 teaspoon curry powder
1 cup finely chopped chutney
2 tablespoons finely snipped chives
   or chopped green onion tops
   Assorted crackers

Advance preparation: Thoroughly beat cheeses, sherry, curry powder, and ½ teaspoon salt with electric mixer. Spread on flat plate, shaping a layer ½ inch thick. Chill till firm.
Before serving: Spread chutney over top. Sprinkle with chives or green onion tops. Serve with crackers. Makes about 3 cups spread.

Turkey-Blue Cheese Ball

1 cup ground cooked turkey
½ cup creamy blue cheese
   salad dressing
3 tablespoons bacon-flavored protein
   bits
¼ cup finely chopped pecans
   Assorted crackers

Advance preparation: Combine turkey, salad dressing, and protein bits. Chill well.
Before serving: Form into a ball. Roll in pecans. Serve with crackers. Makes 1 cup.

Crab-Cream Cheese Special

1 3-ounce package cream cheese,
   softened
¼ cup milk
2 teaspoons lemon juice
1 teaspoon Worcestershire sauce
1 small clove garlic, minced
1 7½-ounce can crab meat, drained,
   finely flaked, and cartilage
   removed
   Assorted crackers

Beat together cream cheese and milk till smooth. Stir in lemon juice, Worcestershire sauce, garlic, dash salt, and dash pepper. Stir in crab meat. Chill till ready to serve. Serve with assorted crackers. Makes 1¾ cups dip.

Olive and Cheese Dip

1 8-ounce package cream cheese,
   softened
1 2¼-ounce can deviled ham
3 tablespoons milk
1 teaspoon finely chopped onion
1 teaspoon Worcestershire sauce
¼ teaspoon dry mustard
3 tablespoons chopped pimiento-stuffed
   green olives
   Sliced pimiento-stuffed green olives
   Potato chips or vegetable dippers

In mixing bowl beat cream cheese, ham, milk, onion, Worcestershire, and dry mustard with electric mixer till fluffy. Fold in the chopped olives. Chill till ready to serve. If necessary, thin with additional milk. Garnish with sliced olives. Serve with potato chips or vegetables. Makes 1½ cups dip.

Triple Cheese Spread

Bring 2 cups shredded sharp Cheddar cheese, one 3-ounce package cream cheese, and ½ cup crumbled blue cheese to room temperature. In small mixing bowl combine cheeses; beat well. Blend in 2 tablespoons milk. Chill till ready to serve. Serve with assorted crackers. Makes about 2 cups.

Smoky Cheese-Olive Spread

1 8-ounce package cream
   cheese, softened
1 6-ounce roll process cheese
   food with hickory smoke flavor,
   softened
¼ cup sliced pimiento-stuffed green
   olives
   Assorted crackers

Advance preparation: Line a 2-cup mold or bowl with clear plastic wrap or foil. Beat cheeses together till well blended; stir in olives. Turn into mold. Chill 4 hours or overnight. **Before serving:** Unmold. Peel off wrap; smooth surface with small spatula. Serve with crackers. Makes about 1½ cups spread.

Onion and Sour Cream Dip

½ cup dairy sour cream
½ cup mayonnaise or salad dressing
½ cup process cheese spread
1 tablespoon onion soup mix
½ teaspoon Worcestershire sauce
   Vegetable dippers (see tip, page 36)

In small mixing bowl combine all ingredients *except* vegetables. Beat with electric mixer till smooth. Chill till ready to serve. Serve with vegetable dippers. Makes 1½ cups dip.

Chili Pepper Spread

2 cups shredded sharp Cheddar
   cheese (8 ounces)
¼ cup milk
2 tablespoons butter or margarine
1 clove garlic, minced
½ cup chopped canned chili peppers
   Assorted crackers

Advance preparation: Bring Cheddar cheese to room temperature. Heat milk to boiling; pour over cheese in mixing bowl. Beat with electric mixer till nearly smooth. Add butter and garlic; beat well. Stir in chopped chili peppers. (Mixture will be thin.) Chill well. Serve with crackers. Makes 1½ cups spread.

Collection of Tidbits

Chicken-Filled Biscuits

1 5-ounce can boned chicken, drained
1 3-ounce package cream cheese with
    pimientos, softened
1 tablespoon sliced green onion with
    tops
    Dash Worcestershire sauce
1 package refrigerated biscuits
    (10 biscuits)

Chop chicken; combine with cream cheese, onion, and Worcestershire. On lightly floured surface roll and stretch each biscuit to a 4-inch circle. Moisten edges with water. Place a rounded tablespoon of chicken mixture in center of each biscuit circle. Fold up 3 sides and pinch edges to seal. Bake on lightly greased baking sheet at 400° till golden, 8 to 10 minutes. Serve warm. Makes 10 snacks.

Pizza Roll-Ups

2 packages refrigerated crescent rolls
    (16 rolls)
1 8-ounce can tomato sauce with onion
1 cup diced salami or pepperoni
½ cup shredded mozzarella cheese
½ teaspoon dried oregano, crushed

Unroll the rolls; press perforations together between triangles to form eight rectangles. Mix remaining ingredients. Place a spoonful of filling along long side of each dough rectangle. Roll up jelly-roll fashion, starting with long side. Seal. Cut in half; place, seam side down, on greased baking sheet. Bake at 375° till golden, about 15 minutes. Makes 16.

Good-to-nibble snacks

← Satisfy your urge to snack with warm *Chicken-Filled Biscuits*, flaky *Seeded Snack Sticks* (see recipe, page 45), or onion-flavored *Noodle-Cereal Snack*.

Noodle-Cereal Snack

2 cups tiny pretzels
1 3-ounce can chow mein noodles
1 cup puffed corn cereal
¼ cup butter or margarine, melted
2 teaspoons Worcestershire sauce
½ teaspoon onion salt
¼ teaspoon garlic powder

In large bowl mix first 3 ingredients. Combine remaining ingredients; pour over pretzel mixture, stirring to coat. Spread in baking pan. Heat at 350° for 5 minutes. Makes 4 cups.

Tortilla-Salami Roll-Ups

8 canned or frozen tortillas
    Horseradish mustard
1 8-ounce package sliced salami *or*
    bologna (8 slices)
4 slices Swiss cheese, cut in half
    (4 ounces)

Thaw frozen tortillas. Spread tortillas with mustard. Place one slice salami atop each tortilla; top with a half-slice cheese. Roll up jelly-roll fashion; secure with wooden picks. Place on wire rack; set rack on baking sheet. Bake at 350° till golden brown and blistery, 10 to 15 minutes. Makes 8 roll-ups.

Curried Corn Snacks

¼ cup butter or margarine
½ to 1 teaspoon curry powder
¼ teaspoon onion salt
⅛ teaspoon ground ginger
2 cups bite-size shredded corn squares
2 cups puffed corn cereal

In large skillet melt butter. Blend in curry, onion salt, and ginger. Add corn squares and cereal; toss to coat. Heat 15 minutes over low heat, stirring frequently. Makes 4 cups.

Toasted Cereal Mix

    2 cups puffed oat cereal
    2 cups bite-size shredded wheat
        squares
    1½ cups peanuts
    1½ cups Cheddar cheese-seasoned
        croutons
    1 cup pretzel sticks
    ½ cup cooking oil
    2 teaspoons Worcestershire sauce
    1 teaspoon garlic powder
    ⅛ teaspoon onion salt
        Several dashes bottled hot pepper
        sauce

In 13x9x2-inch baking pan combine puffed oat cereal, wheat squares, peanuts, croutons, and pretzel sticks. Mix together cooking oil, Worcestershire, garlic powder, onion salt, and hot pepper sauce; pour over cereal mixture. Mix well. Heat in 275° oven about 30 minutes, stirring occasionally. Makes 8 cups mix.

Orange Crunchies

    2 tablespoons butter or margarine,
        melted
    2 teaspoons shredded orange peel
    2 cups bite-size shredded rice squares
    3 tablespoons sugar

In medium skillet combine butter or margarine and orange peel. Add rice squares; toss lightly to coat. Sprinkle with the sugar and again toss gently. Heat over low heat for 5 minutes, stirring once or twice, till cereal is crisp. Turn out on paper toweling. Makes 2 cups.

Hot Roasted Peanuts

    1 pound raw peanuts
    1 tablespoon peanut oil
    1 teaspoon salt

In mixing bowl combine peanuts, peanut oil, and salt. Spread in 13x9x2-inch baking pan. Roast in 350° oven till peanuts are lightly browned and slightly dry to taste, 30 minutes; shake pan occasionally. Makes 3 cups.

Soy Nuts

    1 cup dry soybeans
    3 cups water
    1 teaspoon cooking oil
    ¼ teaspoon salt

Advance preparation: Soak soybeans in water overnight in the refrigerator. Drain soybeans and dry with paper toweling. Spread soybeans in 13x9x2-inch baking pan. Roast soybeans in 300° oven for 2 hours, stirring occasionally. Place under broiler, 3 to 4 inches from heat, and continue to cook, stirring frequently, until soybeans are browned and "popped," 4 to 5 minutes. Toss soybeans with cooking oil and salt. Makes 3 cups.

Double Peanut Snack Mix

Children will like this peanut flavored snack—

    4 cups sweet shredded oat cereal
    1 cup peanuts
    ¼ cup butter or margarine
    ¼ cup creamy peanut butter
    1 teaspoon ground cinnamon

In large bowl combine cereal and peanuts. Heat butter, peanut butter, and cinnamon over low heat till butter and peanut butter are melted. Stir till blended. Slowly pour over cereal mixture, mixing well. Place in 13x9x2-inch baking pan. Heat in 350° oven 10 to 12 minutes; stir occasionally. Cool. Makes 4 cups.

Peppery Pecans

    3 tablespoons butter or margarine
    2 teaspoons Worcestershire sauce
    ¼ teaspoon bottled hot pepper sauce
        Dash pepper
    2 cups pecan halves
        Salt (optional)

In small saucepan melt butter; stir in Worcestershire sauce, hot pepper sauce, and pepper. Add pecan halves, stirring to coat. Spread in shallow baking pan. Heat in 300° oven for 20 minutes, stirring often. Sprinkle with salt, if desired. Serve warm. Makes 2 cups.

Deviled Popcorn

Combine ½ cup melted butter or margarine, 1½ teaspoons chili powder, ½ teaspoon garlic salt, and ⅛ teaspoon cayenne. Pour over 12 cups popped corn, tossing to coat. Makes 12 cups.

Molasses Popcorn

Coated popcorn mixture pictured on page 32 —

> 8 cups popped corn
> 1 cup Spanish peanuts
> 1 cup sugar
> ½ cup water
> ¼ cup molasses
> 1 tablespoon vinegar
> 1 tablespoon butter or margarine
> 1 teaspoon vanilla

Combine popped corn and peanuts; keep warm in 225° oven. In 1½-quart saucepan combine sugar, water, molasses, vinegar, and dash salt. Place over medium heat; cover and heat to boiling. Uncover and cook till soft-crack stage (272° on candy thermometer). Stir in butter and vanilla. Pour slowly over corn mixture, mixing well. Makes 8 cups.

Caramel Crunch

Sweet popcorn and nut snack shown on the cover —

> 8 cups popped corn
> 1 cup pecan halves, toasted
> 1 cup slivered almonds, toasted
> 1⅓ cups sugar
> 1 cup butter or margarine
> ½ cup light corn syrup
> 1 teaspoon vanilla

Combine popped corn and nuts; keep warm in 225° oven. In saucepan combine sugar, butter, and corn syrup. Bring to boiling over medium heat, stirring constantly. Cook and stir till mixture turns caramel color (about 280° on candy thermometer). Remove from heat; stir in vanilla. Place popped corn mixture in buttered 13x9x2-inch baking pan; carefully pour sugar mixture over. Mix well; turn out. Quickly break into clusters with two forks. Store in tightly covered container. Makes about 9 cups.

Marshmallow Popcorn Balls

> 12 cups popped corn
> 6 tablespoons butter or margarine
> 3 cups tiny marshmallows
> ½ of a 3-ounce package raspberry-
>   flavored gelatin (3 tablespoons)

Keep popped corn warm in 225° oven. In saucepan melt butter over medium-low heat. Add marshmallows; stir till melted. Blend in gelatin. Pour over popped corn, mixing well. With buttered hands, form into balls. Makes 12 medium (3-inch) or 18 small (2-inch) balls.

Peanut Butter Popcorn Balls

> 6 cups popped corn
> ½ cup sugar
> ½ cup light corn syrup
> ½ cup chunk-style peanut butter
> ½ teaspoon vanilla

Lightly salt the popped corn; keep warm in 225° oven. In small saucepan combine sugar and corn syrup; cook and stir over medium heat just till mixture comes to full rolling boil, 3 to 4 minutes. Remove from heat; stir in peanut butter and vanilla. Immediately pour over warm popped corn, mixing well. With well-buttered hands, form into balls, using about ½ cup mixture for each. Makes 8 to 10.

Cinnamon Popcorn Balls

> 12 cups popped corn
> 1 cup sugar
> ⅔ cup red cinnamon candies
> 1 tablespoon vinegar
> 1 or 2 drops oil of cinnamon

Keep popped corn warm in 225° oven. Butter sides of a medium saucepan. In saucepan combine sugar, red cinnamon candies, vinegar, ⅔ cup water, and ¼ teaspoon salt. Cook till hard-ball stage (250° on candy thermometer), stirring till sugar and candies dissolve. Stir in oil of cinnamon. Pour slowly over popped corn, mixing well. With buttered hands, form into 2½-inch balls. Makes about 14 balls.

Popcorn Crisp

> 16 cups popped corn
> 1½ cups peanuts
> 1 cup raisins
> 2 cups honey
> 1 tablespoon vinegar
> 1 tablespoon butter or margarine

Combine popped corn, peanuts, and raisins. In 3-quart saucepan cook honey, vinegar, and butter over medium-low heat till soft-crack stage (290° on candy thermometer). Pour honey mixture over corn mixture. When cool enough to handle, press into buttered 15½x 10½x1-inch baking pan; cut in squares. Makes about 72 pieces.

Cake and Berry Skewers

> ½ cup light corn syrup
> 1 tablespoon orange liqueur
> 1 loaf-size angel cake, cut into 1½-inch cubes
> 1 3½-ounce can flaked coconut
> Fresh whole strawberries

Mix corn syrup and liqueur. Spear cake cube with fork; dip in syrup mixture, then roll in coconut. Repeat with remaining cake. Alternately thread cake and berries on small skewers. Broil on foil-lined broiler pan 2 to 3 inches from heat till coconut is toasted, 7 to 9 minutes. Turn often, using a fork to help turn cake cubes. Makes about 6 servings.

Butterscotch-Cereal Bars

> 1 3¾- or 4-ounce package *regular* butterscotch pudding mix
> ½ cup light corn syrup
> ½ cup chunk-style peanut butter
> 4 cups puffed oat cereal

In large saucepan combine pudding mix and corn syrup. Heat to boiling over medium heat, stirring constantly. Boil ½ minute. Remove from heat; blend in peanut butter. Add cereal, stirring till coated. Turn into greased 9x9x2-inch pan. Cool; cut into bars. Makes 18 bars.

Liver-Filled Crescents

> 1 package refrigerated crescent rolls (8 rolls)
> 1 4¾-ounce can liver spread
> 2 teaspoons Dijon-style mustard *or* 1 teaspoon lemon juice
> ¼ teaspoon celery seed *or* ¼ teaspoon garlic powder

Unroll the rolls and separate into four rectangles. Pinch perforations to seal. Cut each rectangle lengthwise and crosswise to form four smaller rectangles. Combine liver spread with *either* the mustard and celery seed *or* with the lemon juice and garlic powder. Place a generous teaspoon of mixture on half of each rectangle. Fold other half over; seal edges. Bake on lightly greased baking sheet at 350° for 10 to 12 minutes. Makes 16.

Toasted Pumpkin Seed

> 2 cups shelled pumpkin seed
> 1 tablespoon cooking oil
> 1 teaspoon salt

Combine pumpkin seed, cooking oil, and salt. Spread mixture in shallow baking pan. Toast in 350° oven for 15 minutes, stirring once or twice. Drain on paper toweling. Store in covered container. Makes 2 cups.

Think nutrition

You can eat between meals and still practice good nutrition. To make snacks work for you nutritionally, select foods that help supply required nutrients. Cheeses, for example, provide protein and other nutrients. Apples, oranges, carrots, cherry tomatoes, and other fruits and vegetables contribute vitamins. Milk, ice cream, and snacks made with milk supply calcium (needed for strong teeth and bones). And hearty cold cuts and fully cooked sausages are good sources of protein.

Caraway-Cheese Stack-Ups

    1 3-ounce package cream
        cheese, softened
    1 2¼-ounce can deviled ham
    ¼ teaspoon caraway seed
    ¼ teaspoon grated onion
    6 slices American cheese

Advance preparation: Mix first 4 ingredients. Spread *half* of mixture on *two slices* American cheese. Stack, filling sides up; top with third slice cheese. Repeat with remaining ham mixture and cheese slices. Wrap; chill.
Before serving: Cut cheese stacks in half. Cut each half into eight triangles. Serve on wooden picks. Makes 32 triangles.

Cheese Wafers

    1 cup grated sharp American cheese
    1 cup all-purpose flour
    ⅛ teaspoon paprika
    ½ cup butter or margarine

Combine cheese, flour, and paprika. Cut in butter till like coarse meal. With hands, work into smooth dough. On a floured surface, roll dough to 10x9 inch rectangle, about ¼ inch thick. Cut with a 2-inch fluted round cookie cutter. Bake on *ungreased* baking sheet at 425° for 8 to 9 minutes; cool. Makes 40.

Cheese Snacks

    1 6-ounce roll sharp process cheese
        food
    ½ cup butter or margarine, softened
    1½ cups all-purpose flour
    ⅛ teaspoon cayenne
    ¾ cup finely crushed cornflakes

Beat cheese food and butter together. Combine flour and cayenne; add to cheese mixture with cornflakes. Mix well. Roll to 10x8-inch rectangle between sheets of waxed paper. Remove top paper; cut into 1-inch squares. Bake squares on *ungreased* baking sheet at 325° till lightly browned, 15 to 17 minutes. Cool. Store in tightly covered container. Makes 64.

Cheeses are ideal for snacking. Clockwise from top: Edam, Crema Danica, Gruyère, La Grappe, Brie, a process cheese, Port du Salut, and Gorgonzola.

Seeded Snack Sticks

Flaky pastry snacks shown on page 40 —

    4 frozen patty shells
    1 slightly beaten egg yolk
    1 tablespoon milk
    ¼ teaspoon onion salt
    3 tablespoons shelled sunflower seed,
        coarsely chopped
    2 tablespoons sesame seed, toasted
    1 tablespoon poppy seed

Thaw patty shells in refrigerator for 2 hours. On lightly floured cloth arrange patty shells in a square, overlapping edges slightly. Roll to a 12x12-inch square. Cut in thirds. Combine egg yolk, milk, and onion salt. Brush over pastry. Sprinkle *each third* of the pastry with a different kind of seed. Cut each pastry portion into 3x1-inch strips. Place strips on *ungreased* baking sheet. Bake at 400° for 8 to 10 minutes. Makes 48 sticks.

Mini-Meal Sandwiches

Meatball Sandwiches

2 slightly beaten eggs
3 tablespoons milk
½ cup fine dry bread crumbs
¾ teaspoon salt
1 pound ground beef
½ pound bulk Italian pork sausage
½ cup chopped onion
½ cup chopped green pepper
1 8-ounce can tomato sauce (1 cup)
1 6-ounce can tomato paste
2 teaspoons sugar
1 teaspoon garlic salt
½ teaspoon dried oregano, crushed
¼ teaspoon dried parsley flakes,
    crushed
8 individual French rolls

Combine eggs, milk, crumbs, salt, and ⅛ teaspoon pepper; add beef and mix well. Form into twenty-four 1½-inch meatballs. Brown in hot skillet; remove meatballs. In same skillet combine sausage, onion, and green pepper; cook till sausage is browned. Drain fat. Stir in tomato sauce, tomato paste, sugar, garlic salt, oregano, parsley flakes, and 1 cup water. Return meatballs to skillet. Cover; simmer 15 minutes, stirring once or twice. Cut thin slice from tops of rolls; hollow out rolls, leaving a ¼-inch wall. Fill each roll with 3 meatballs and some of the sauce. Makes 8 sandwiches.

Cheese-Chili Burgers

4 hamburger buns, split and toasted
1 10½-ounce can chili without beans
¼ cup sour cream dip with French onion
4 slices American cheese

Spread bottom of *each* toasted bun with ¼ *cup* chili. Top *each* with *1 tablespoon* sour cream dip. Broil till heated through, 4 to 5 minutes. Top each sandwich with one cheese slice and broil till cheese melts, 1 minute more. Cover with bun tops. Makes 4 sandwiches.

Pizza Rustica

1 14-ounce package pizza mix
½ cup finely diced salami
½ cup finely diced boiled ham
½ cup finely diced bologna
½ cup shredded mozzarella cheese
½ cup cream-style cottage cheese

Combine packets of flour and herbs from pizza mix. Prepare dough according to package directions. On waxed paper, roll dough to 18x8-inch rectangle. Combine salami, ham, bologna, and cheeses; spread over dough. Carefully roll up jelly-roll fashion, starting with long side. Cut into six 3-inch rolls. Place, seam side down, on greased baking sheet. Bake at 425° till golden, about 12 minutes. Heat pizza sauce from mix; pass with rolls. Serves 6.

Saucy Beef Buns

1 pound ground beef
¼ cup finely chopped celery
¼ cup chopped onion
1 10½-ounce can condensed chicken
    gumbo soup
¼ cup hot-style catsup
1 teaspoon prepared mustard
8 hamburger buns, split
¾ cup shredded Swiss cheese

In skillet cook beef, celery, and onion till meat is browned; drain off excess fat. Stir in soup, catsup, and mustard. Cook and stir till bubbly. Spoon ¼ *cup* mixture onto bottom half of *each* bun. Top *each* with about *1½ tablespoons* cheese; replace tops. Makes 8.

Italian-style sandwiches

Fresh rolls form the base for tomato and meat-sauced →
Meatball Sandwiches. Serve rolled-up *Pizza Rustica* with heated sauce from packaged pizza mix.

Dilly Frank and Egg Rolls

6 frankfurters
2 hard-cooked eggs, chopped
¼ cup sliced green onion
¼ cup mayonnaise or salad dressing
1 teaspoon prepared mustard
1 teaspoon vinegar
¾ teaspoon dried dillweed
¼ teaspoon salt
6 frankfurter buns, split
  Butter or margarine, softened

Advance preparation: Slice frankfurters crosswise in ⅛-inch-thick slices. Combine chopped hard-cooked eggs, sliced green onion, mayonnaise or salad dressing, prepared mustard, vinegar, dillweed, and salt. Stir in sliced frankfurters. Spread frankfurter buns with softened butter or margarine. On bottom of buns spread frankfurter mixture; replace tops. Wrap in foil, label, and freeze up to 2 weeks.
Before serving: Place frozen, wrapped sandwiches on baking sheet. Bake at 350° till heated through, about 40 minutes. Makes 6.

Swiss-Olive Sandwiches

4 slices bacon
1 cup shredded Swiss cheese
  (4 ounces)
1 slightly beaten egg
2 tablespoons chopped pimiento-
  stuffed green olives
¼ teaspoon paprika
  • • •
2 ½-inch-thick slices round rye bread
  Butter or margarine, softened
  Sliced pimiento-stuffed green olives

Cook bacon till crisp; drain off fat. Crumble bacon and set aside. Combine shredded Swiss cheese, egg, 2 tablespoons chopped olives, and paprika. Spread one side of rye bread with softened butter or margarine. Spread Swiss cheese mixture on bread to edges. Sprinkle with crumbled bacon. Place sandwiches on baking sheet. Bake at 350° till heated through, 12 to 15 minutes. Garnish with sliced pimiento-stuffed green olives. Cut each sandwich into 6 wedges. Makes 4 servings.

Deviled French-Fried Sandwiches

Tangy sour cream mixture coats these golden brown grilled sandwiches—

8 slices white bread
  Mayonnaise or salad dressing
1 2¼-ounce can deviled ham
4 slices sharp American cheese
  (4 ounces)
4 thin slices onion
  • • •
2 eggs
3 tablespoons dairy sour cream
  Dash salt
  Butter or margarine

Spread *4 slices* white bread lightly with mayonnaise or salad dressing, then with deviled ham. Top with American cheese and onion. Top with remaining white bread. Beat together eggs, dairy sour cream, and salt. Dip each sandwich in egg mixture. In large skillet cook sandwiches in butter or margarine over medium-low heat till golden brown on both sides and cheese is melted. Makes 4 sandwiches.

Salad in a Bun

½ cup mayonnaise
1½ teaspoons snipped parsley
½ teaspoon prepared mustard
¼ teaspoon dried tarragon, crushed
¼ teaspoon dried dillweed
  • • •
4 hamburger buns, split and toasted
  Lettuce
¼ small green pepper, sliced into thin
  strips
1 cup cauliflowerets, thinly sliced
1 tomato, thinly sliced

Advance preparation: In bowl combine mayonnaise, snipped parsley, prepared mustard, tarragon, and dillweed. Cover and refrigerate mayonnaise mixture from 1 to 24 hours.
Before serving: Spread mayonnaise mixture generously on bottom of buns. Top with lettuce, green pepper strips, and cauliflower slices. Sprinkle tomato lightly with salt; arrange over other vegetables. Replace tops of buns; secure with wooden picks. Makes 4 servings.

Hot Ham Sandwiches

½ pound ground fully cooked ham
¾ cup shredded mozzarella cheese
⅓ cup pizza sauce
¼ cup chopped dill pickle
¼ cup finely chopped onion
2 tablespoons diced green pepper
6 hamburger *or* frankfurter buns, split
Butter or margarine, softened

Combine ham, cheese, pizza sauce, pickle, onion, and green pepper. Spread buns with butter. On bottom of *each* bun spread a generous ⅓ *cup* of filling; replace tops of buns. Place on baking sheet. Bake at 350° till heated through, about 20 minutes. Makes 6.

Waldorf-Whole Wheat Sandwiches

Combine one 8-ounce package cream cheese, softened; 1 tablespoon milk; and 2 teaspoons lemon juice. Stir in 1 large apple, finely chopped (1 cup); ½ cup finely snipped pitted dates; and ¼ cup finely chopped walnuts. Spread 16 slices whole wheat bread with softened butter or margarine. On *each* of 8 slices bread spread ¼ *cup* of the filling mixture; top with lettuce and remaining bread. Makes 8.

Avocado-Topped Hamwiches

1 tablespoon lemon juice
1 teaspoon prepared horseradish
Dash bottled hot pepper sauce
⅓ cup mayonnaise or salad dressing
1 medium avocado, peeled and pitted
10 slices rye bread
Lettuce
5 slices Swiss cheese
10 slices boiled ham
1 medium tomato, cut in 10 wedges

Mix juice, horseradish, hot pepper sauce, and ¼ teaspoon salt. Fold in mayonnaise. Cut avocado into 10 slices. Atop *each* of *5 slices* bread place lettuce, cheese slice, 2 rolled boiled ham slices, 2 tomato wedges, and 2 avocado slices. Drizzle with mayonnaise mixture. Top with remaining bread. Makes 5.

Tuna-Cream Cheese Sandwiches

1 6½- or 7-ounce can tuna, drained and flaked
2 hard-cooked eggs, coarsely chopped
2 tablespoons finely chopped dill pickle
2 tablespoons chopped green onion
1 3-ounce package cream cheese, softened
2 tablespoons mayonnaise or salad dressing
1 teaspoon lemon juice
¼ teaspoon salt
12 slices Vienna bread
Butter or margarine, softened
Lettuce

Stir together flaked tuna, chopped hard-cooked eggs, dill pickle, and green onion. Blend together cream cheese, mayonnaise or salad dressing, lemon juice, and salt; stir into tuna mixture. Spread Vienna bread slices with butter or margarine. Spread tuna mixture on 6 slices bread; top with lettuce and the remaining slices of Vienna bread. Makes 6 sandwiches.

A tangy mayonnaise dressing adds the finishing touch to decorative *Avocado-Topped Hamwiches*. This colorful sandwich goes well with fresh fruit.

Enticing Sweets

Rocky Road Candy

2 8-ounce bars milk chocolate
3 cups tiny marshmallows
¾ cup coarsely broken walnuts

In medium saucepan slowly melt chocolate over low heat, stirring constantly. Remove from heat; beat till smooth. Stir in marshmallows and nuts. Spread in buttered 8x8x2-inch baking pan. If necessary, chill to firm chocolate. Cut in squares. Makes 1½ pounds candy.

Snowballs

Combine one 6-ounce package semisweet chocolate pieces and ⅓ cup evaporated milk. Heat and stir over low heat till chocolate melts. Remove from heat. Stir in 1¼ cups sifted powdered sugar and ½ cup chopped walnuts. Chill a few minutes. Form into 1-inch balls; roll in 1⅓ cups flaked coconut. Makes about 30.

Peanut Butter Logs

1 cup chunk-style peanut butter
2 tablespoons butter or margarine
1¼ cups sifted powdered sugar
3 cups crisp rice cereal
Chopped peanuts

Advance preparation: Blend peanut butter and butter; stir in sugar. Add cereal; mix well, crushing cereal slightly. Shape in three 7x1¼-inch logs. Cover with nuts. Wrap; chill firm. **Before serving:** Carefully cut in ½-inch-thick slices. Makes 1 pound candy.

Treasury of candy favorites

← Try these tempting candies—marshmallow-filled *Rocky Road Candy*, coconut-coated *Snowballs*, *Toffee-Butter Crunch*, and *Kris Kringles*.

Kris Kringles

1 6-ounce package semisweet chocolate pieces (1 cup)
2 tablespoons butter or margarine
1 egg
1 cup sifted powdered sugar
½ teaspoon vanilla
½ cup flaked coconut
½ cup chopped dry roasted peanuts

Advance preparation: In medium saucepan melt chocolate and butter or margarine over low heat, stirring constantly. Remove from heat; cool to lukewarm. Beat in egg till smooth and glossy. Add powdered sugar, vanilla, and dash salt; mix well. Stir in coconut and peanuts. Chill. Form into a 10-inch-long roll. Wrap and chill till firm, several hours or overnight. **Before serving:** Slice chilled chocolate-nut roll ¼ inch thick. Makes 40 slices candy.

Toffee-Butter Crunch

1 cup butter or margarine
1⅓ cups sugar
1 tablespoon light corn syrup
1 cup coarsely chopped blanched almonds, toasted
2 8-ounce bars milk chocolate, melted
1 cup finely chopped blanched almonds, toasted

In large saucepan melt butter. Add sugar, corn syrup, and 3 tablespoons water. Cook over medium heat, stirring occasionally, till hard-crack stage (300° on candy thermometer). Quickly stir in 1 cup coarsely chopped almonds. Spread in well-greased 13x9x2-inch baking pan. Cool well. Turn out on waxed paper. Spread with *half* the chocolate; sprinkle with ½ *cup* finely chopped almonds. Cover with waxed paper; invert. Spread with remaining chocolate; sprinkle with remaining almonds. If necessary, chill to firm chocolate. Break into pieces. Makes about 60 pieces.

Cereal Candy Balls

A sweet snack that is also nutritious —

In 2-quart saucepan combine ½ cup honey and 2 tablespoons packed brown sugar. Cook till hard-ball stage (250° on candy thermometer). Pour over 3 cups granola cereal, stirring just to mix well. Oil hands lightly; shape cereal mixture into 1-inch balls. Makes 30 candies.

Candymaking tests

For success with cooked candies, use a candy thermometer or the cold water test.

If using a candy thermometer, first check it in boiling water. If thermometer does not register 212°F, add or subtract the same number of degrees in the recipe. Clip thermometer to pan after candy mixture boils, then read at eye level. Make sure bulb is covered with candy mixture but does not touch bottom of pan.

For the cold water test, drop hot candy mixture from spoon into small bowl of cold water. With fingers, form into ball. Use the following guides: *soft-ball* (234-240°F) — ball flattens when removed from water; *firm-ball* (244-248°) — ball does not flatten when removed; *hard-ball* (250-266°) — ball is hard, yet pliable; *soft-crack* (270-290°) — separates into non-brittle threads; and *hard-crack* (300-310°) — separates into hard, brittle threads.

Homemade Gumdrops

Colorful candies pictured on pages 32 and 33 —

> 1 1¾-ounce package powdered fruit pectin
> ½ teaspoon baking soda
> ¾ cup water
> 1 cup sugar
> 1 cup light corn syrup
> Flavoring*
> Sugar

Advance preparation: In 2-quart saucepan combine pectin and baking soda. Stir in water (mixture will be foamy). In another 2-quart saucepan mix the 1 cup sugar and corn syrup. Place both pans over high heat. Cook and stir till foam is thinned from the pectin mixture and the sugar mixture is boiling rapidly, 3 to 5 minutes. Pour pectin mixture in a slow, steady stream into boiling sugar mixture, stirring constantly, about 1 minute. Cook and stir 1 minute more. Remove from heat; add desired Flavoring*. Pour into buttered 9x5x3-inch loaf pan. Cool till firm, about 2 hours.

*Flavorings: For Orange Gumdrops, stir in 7 drops yellow food coloring, 1 drop red food coloring, and 2 teaspoons orange extract. For Lemon Gumdrops, stir in 10 drops yellow food coloring and 2 teaspoons lemon extract. For Cherry Gumdrops, stir in 7 drops red food coloring and 1 teaspoon cherry extract. For Mint Gumdrops, stir in 7 drops green food coloring and 1 teaspoon mint extract.

Before serving: Cut candy in ¾-inch squares; roll each in sugar. Store in loosely covered container. Makes about 55 gumdrops.

Almond Caramels

Butter bottom and sides of 9x5x3-inch loaf pan. In 2-quart saucepan combine 1 cup granulated sugar, ½ cup packed brown sugar, and ½ cup light corn syrup. Add 1½ cups light cream and ¼ cup butter. Cook and stir over medium heat till sugars dissolve. Continue cooking, stirring occasionally, till firm-ball stage (248° on candy thermometer). Remove from heat; add 1 teaspoon vanilla. Stir in ½ cup chopped almonds, toasted. Turn into loaf pan; cool. Cut in squares; wrap. Makes 36.

Marshmallow Squares

Chewy homemade candies shown on page 33—

2 cups granulated sugar
3 envelopes unflavored gelatin
⅛ teaspoon salt
1 cup water
1 teaspoon vanilla
Powdered sugar

In medium saucepan combine granulated sugar, gelatin, and salt; stir in water. Heat till sugar dissolves, then bring just to a boil. Remove from heat; cool slightly, about 5 minutes. Stir in vanilla. Transfer to large mixing bowl. Beat at high speed of electric mixer till mixture resembles thick marshmallow creme, about 10 minutes. Pour into buttered 13x9x2-inch baking pan. Cool. With kitchen shears dipped in hot water, cut in 1¼-inch squares. Roll in powdered sugar. Makes about 72 pieces.

Fudge Bars

¼ cup butter or margarine
1 cup packed brown sugar
1 cup grated coconut
½ cup chopped walnuts
1 5⅓-ounce can evaporated milk
1 8-ounce package cream cheese, softened
1 egg
2 cups chocolate fudge frosting mix (½ of 2-layer-size package)
1 roll refrigerated chocolate chip cookie dough

Advance preparation: Line 13x9x2-inch baking pan with foil. Melt butter in foil-lined pan. Sprinkle brown sugar, coconut, and nuts over butter. Drizzle evaporated milk over all. In small mixing bowl beat cream cheese and egg till smooth. Gradually add frosting mix to cheese mixture; blend well. Carefully spread cheese mixture over coconut mixture in pan. Slice cookie dough into ¼-inch-thick slices; arrange slices over cheese mixture. Bake at 350° till golden brown, 35 to 40 minutes. Immediately invert on cookie sheet to remove from pan. Chill thoroughly.
Before serving: Cut into bars. Makes 36 bars.

Nutty Chocolate Candy Cookies

1½ cups semisweet chocolate pieces
¾ cup sugar
¼ cup butter or margarine
1 egg
1½ teaspoons vanilla
• • •
½ cup all-purpose flour
½ teaspoon salt
¼ teaspoon baking powder
½ cup chopped walnuts

In small saucepan melt *1 cup* of the chocolate pieces over low heat; cool. In small mixing bowl cream together sugar and butter or margarine. Add egg and vanilla; beat well. Blend in melted chocolate. Stir flour, salt, and baking powder together thoroughly. Add to creamed mixture, mixing well. Stir in walnuts and remaining chocolate pieces. Drop dough from teaspoon, 2 inches apart, onto lightly greased cookie sheet. Bake at 350° for 8 to 10 minutes. Makes about 30 cookies.

Whole Wheat-Fruit Drop Cookies

½ cup butter or margarine
½ cup granulated sugar
⅓ cup packed brown sugar
1 egg
½ teaspoon vanilla
1 cup whole wheat flour
½ teaspoon baking powder
¼ teaspoon baking soda
¼ teaspoon salt
¾ cup quick-cooking rolled oats
½ cup snipped pitted dates
½ cup raisins
½ cup chopped walnuts
½ cup flaked coconut
1½ teaspoons grated orange peel

Cream together butter and sugars till light and fluffy. Beat in egg and vanilla. Stir whole wheat flour, baking powder, soda, and salt together thoroughly. Stir into creamed mixture; mix well. Stir in oats, dates, raisins, nuts, coconut, and peel. Drop from teaspoon, 2 inches apart, onto greased cookie sheet. Bake at 375° for 10 to 12 minutes. Makes 48 cookies.

Molasses-Peanut Butter Cookies

½ cup shortening
½ cup sugar
½ cup light molasses
½ cup chunk-style peanut butter
1 egg
2 cups all-purpose flour
¼ teaspoon baking powder
¼ teaspoon baking soda

Cream together shortening and sugar; beat in molasses, peanut butter, and egg. Stir flour, baking powder, soda, and ¼ teaspoon salt together. Stir into peanut butter mixture. Drop by rounded teaspoonfuls, 2 inches apart, onto *ungreased* cookie sheet. Flatten slightly with fork. Bake at 375° about 8 minutes. Makes 48.

Butterscotch Crunch Sundaes

1 3-ounce can chow mein
   noodles (2 cups)
1½ cups chopped peanuts
½ gallon vanilla ice cream
1 12-ounce package butterscotch pieces
½ cup light corn syrup
¼ cup butter or margarine

Advance preparation: Crush noodles; mix with peanuts. Scoop 12 ice cream balls onto baking sheet. Quickly roll balls in peanut mixture till coated; return to sheet. Freeze firm.
Before serving: Mix butterscotch pieces, corn syrup, butter, and ½ cup water. Bring to a boil. Cook and stir 1 minute; cool. Spoon some sauce into 12 dishes; place an ice cream ball in each. Drizzle with remaining sauce. Makes 12 servings.

Hidden Treasure Sundaes

1 pint vanilla ice cream
½ cup jam *or* jelly
¼ cup flaked coconut

Advance preparation: Soften ice cream slightly. In four 9-ounce paper cold drink cups alternate layers of ice cream and jam. Top with jam and coconut. Freeze firm. Serves 4.

Candied Ginger Sundae Sauce

½ cup sugar
¼ cup orange-flavored breakfast drink
   powder
2 tablespoons cornstarch
2 tablespoons finely snipped candied
   ginger
Dash salt
1½ cups water
2 tablespoons butter or margarine

In saucepan mix sugar, drink powder, cornstarch, ginger, and salt. Gradually blend in water. Bring to a boil; cook 2 minutes, stirring constantly. Remove from heat; blend in butter. Cool. If desired, store in refrigerator; stir well before serving. Makes 1¾ cups.

Hot Fudge-Peanut Butter Sauce

Serve warm on ice cream or pound cake à la mode —

1 6-ounce package semisweet chocolate
   pieces (1 cup)
1 cup milk
½ cup sugar
½ cup peanut butter

In small saucepan combine chocolate, milk, and sugar. Bring to boiling, stirring constantly. Gradually stir peanut butter into chocolate mixture. Serve warm. Makes 2 cups sauce.

Peach Parfaits

Golden layered parfaits pictured on page 32 —

¼ cup sugar
1 tablespoon cornstarch
1 cup orange juice
1 large peach, peeled and sliced
½ cup seedless green grapes, halved
1 quart pineapple sherbet

Advance preparation: Combine sugar and cornstarch; stir in orange juice. Add fruits; cook and stir till thickened. Simmer till peaches are just tender, 2 to 3 minutes. Cool; chill.
Before serving: Layer fruit mixture and sherbet in 8 parfait glasses. If desired, garnish with additional peach slices. Makes 8 parfaits.

Caramel-Nut Apples

Caramel apples are rolled in crunchy walnuts —

1 cup packed brown sugar
½ cup light corn syrup
¼ cup butter or margarine
½ of a 14-ounce can *sweetened condensed* **milk (⅔ cup)**
½ teaspoon vanilla
6 wooden sticks
6 medium apples
½ cup chopped walnuts

Advance preparation: In saucepan combine brown sugar, light corn syrup, and butter or margarine. Bring mixture to boiling over medium heat, stirring constantly. Stir in sweetened condensed milk. Simmer, stirring constantly, till soft-ball stage (234° to 240° on candy thermometer). Stir in vanilla; remove from heat. Insert a wooden stick into blossom end of each apple. Dip apple in caramel mixture, turning till apple is completely coated. Immediately roll bottom half of coated apple in chopped walnuts. Repeat with remaining apples. Place on baking sheet covered with waxed paper. Chill till caramel is firm. Makes 6.

Frozen Chocolate Sticks

Coconut-covered sweets shown on pages 32 and 33 —

1 3¾- or 4-ounce package *regular* **chocolate pudding mix**
¼ cup sugar
2 egg yolks
2 stiffly beaten egg whites
6 wooden sticks
Flaked coconut

Advance preparation: In saucepan combine pudding mix and sugar; prepare according to the package directions. Stir a moderate amount of hot pudding into egg yolks; return to remaining pudding in pan. Cook and stir till thickened and bubbly. Cover surface with waxed paper; cool. Fold whites into pudding. Spoon into six 5-ounce paper drink cups. Insert wooden stick into each. Freeze firm.
Before serving: Place chocolate sticks under running hot water to melt chocolate slightly; peel off paper. Dip in coconut. Makes 6.

Lemon-Berry Parfaits

2 8-ounce cartons lemon yogurt
1 10-ounce package frozen raspberries, thawed

In 4 parfait glasses alternate layers of yogurt and raspberries. Garnish with whipped cream and candied lemon slice, if desired. Serves 4.

Frosty Dipped Bananas

½ pound milk chocolate
8 wooden sticks
4 bananas, halved crosswise
1½ cups chopped peanuts

Advance preparation: In small, heavy saucepan melt chocolate over very low heat; stir constantly. *Do not add any liquid.* Remove from heat; transfer to shallow dish. Insert wooden sticks into banana halves. Roll in chocolate, then immediately in nuts. Place on baking sheet covered with waxed paper. Freeze. (If not eaten same day, wrap in moisture-vaporproof wrap; store in freezer.) Makes 8.

To coat *Frosty Dipped Bananas,* roll banana halves lightly across the surface of the milk chocolate, then roll in peanuts before the chocolate hardens.

Snacks to Drink

Mexican Mocha Float

2 teaspoons instant coffee granules
¾ cup hot water
3½ cups milk
⅓ cup chocolate syrup
2 tablespoons sugar
½ teaspoon ground cinnamon
Vanilla ice cream

Advance preparation: Dissolve instant coffee in the hot water; add milk, chocolate syrup, sugar, and cinnamon. Stir to blend. Chill.
Before serving: Beat with rotary beater till foamy. Place two scoops of ice cream in each of 6 glasses; fill with milk mixture. Serves 6.

Snow Punch

Garnish each serving with flaked coconut—

½ cup lemon juice
3 ripe bananas
1 cup light cream
½ cup sugar
3 7-ounce bottles lemon-lime
   carbonated beverage, chilled
1 cup lemon sherbet
3 tablespoons flaked coconut

Advance preparation: Pour lemon juice into blender container. Slice bananas into container. Cover; blend till pureed. Combine banana mixture, cream, and sugar; chill.
Before serving: Add lemon-lime carbonated beverage, stirring gently to blend. Serve in small glasses or punch cups. Top with spoonfuls of lemon sherbet; sprinkle with flaked coconut. Makes about 6 cups punch.

Frothy drinkable snacks

← *Mexican Mocha Float,* flavored with coffee, cinnamon, and chocolate syrup, and fresh-tasting, orangy *Fruit Fizz* are cool and refreshing snacks anytime.

Double Raspberry Fizzers

Frothy beverage shown on page 32—

1 10-ounce jar raspberry jam
   Raspberry sherbet
   Vanilla ice cream
2 12-ounce bottles lemon-lime
   carbonated beverage, chilled

Combine jam and ½ cup cold water; mix well. Divide jam mixture among 5 tall glasses, using about ¼ cup for each. Add a scoop of sherbet, then a scoop of ice cream; top with another scoop of sherbet. Carefully fill with carbonated beverage. Makes 5 servings.

White Grape Cooler

1 6-ounce can frozen orange juice
   concentrate
1½ cups white grape juice
¼ cup lemon juice
¼ cup honey
1 12-ounce bottle lemon-lime
   carbonated beverage, chilled
1 pint lemon sherbet

Prepare juice concentrate according to directions on can; stir in white grape juice, lemon juice, and honey. Divide mixture among 6 tall glasses. Add carbonated beverage. Top with scoops of sherbet. Makes 6 servings.

Fruit Fizz

1 cup orange juice, chilled
1 cup vanilla ice cream
1 cup orange *or* lemon sherbet
1 12-ounce bottle lemon-lime
   carbonated beverage, chilled

Place first 3 ingredients in blender container. Cover; blend just till smooth. Pour into 4 tall glasses. Slowly pour in carbonated beverage; stir gently. Serve at once. Serves 4.

Choco-Nutty Shake

  1 cup cold milk
  2 tablespoons chocolate syrup
  2 tablespoons peanut butter
  1 pint vanilla ice cream, softened

In blender container combine milk, chocolate syrup, and peanut butter. Cover and blend till smooth. Add vanilla ice cream by spoonfuls; cover and blend till mixture is smooth. Pour into glasses. Makes 2 or 3 servings.

Spicy Hot Chocolate

  ½ cup sugar
  3 1-ounce squares unsweetened
      chocolate, cut up
  1 teaspoon ground cinnamon
  ¼ teaspoon ground nutmeg
  ¼ teaspoon salt
  1½ cups water
        • • •
  4 cups milk
    Frozen whipped dessert topping,
      thawed

In saucepan combine sugar, unsweetened chocolate, cinnamon, nutmeg, and salt. Stir in water. Cook, stirring constantly, over low heat till chocolate melts. Bring to boiling; reduce heat and simmer 4 minutes, stirring constantly. Add milk; heat over low heat till mixture is hot. Beat with rotary beater till foamy. Serve in mugs or cups. Garnish with whipped dessert topping. Makes 6 servings.

Lemon-Apple Drink

  3 cups apple juice *or* cider, chilled
  1 6-ounce can frozen pink lemonade
      concentrate
    Ice cubes
  1 10-ounce bottle lemon-lime
      carbonated beverage, chilled

Combine apple juice or cider and pink lemonade concentrate; stir till dissolved. Pour over ice cubes in 4 glasses. Fill glasses with carbonated beverage. Makes 4 servings.

Strawberry-Banana Shake

  1 pint strawberry ice cream, softened
  1 cup cold milk
  1 medium banana, mashed (½ cup)

In mixing bowl combine strawberry ice cream, cold milk, and mashed banana. Beat till smooth. Pour into glasses. Serves 2 or 3.

Banana-Chocolate Malt

  1 cup cold milk
  1 banana, cut up
  2 tablespoons plain malted milk powder
  1 pint chocolate ice cream, softened

In blender container combine milk, banana, and malted milk powder. Cover; blend till smooth. Add ice cream by spoonfuls; blend till smooth. Pour into glasses. Serves 2 or 3.

Pineapple Frostea

  2 tablespoons instant tea powder
  3 cups ice water
  ½ of a 6-ounce can frozen pineapple
      juice concentrate (⅓ cup)
  1 pint pineapple sherbet

Dissolve instant tea powder in ice water; stir in frozen juice concentrate till dissolved. Pour pineapple-tea mixture into 6 glasses; add a scoop of pineapple sherbet to each glass. Stir gently. Makes 6 servings.

Cinnamon Iced Coffee

  3½ cups hot strong coffee
  6 inches stick cinnamon
  ½ cup whipping cream
    Cracked ice

Advance preparation: Pour hot coffee over the stick cinnamon; let stand 1 hour. Remove stick cinnamon; stir in cream. Chill well.
Before serving: Pour over cracked ice in glasses. Sweeten to taste. Serve with stick cinnamon stirrers, if desired. Serves 4 or 5.

Citrus Cooler

Especially refreshing on a hot summer afternoon—

> ¾ cup cold water
> 1 6-ounce can orange-grapefruit juice
>   concentrate *or* orange-pineapple
>   juice concentrate, thawed
> 2 pints lemon sherbet
> 1 28-ounce bottle ginger ale, chilled

In blender container combine *half* of the cold water, *half* of the orange-grapefruit or orange-pineapple juice concentrate, and *half* of the lemon sherbet. Cover and blend 15 seconds. Pour into 3 tall glasses. Repeat with remaining water, concentrate, and lemon sherbet. Carefully fill glasses with chilled ginger ale. Stir gently. Makes 6 servings.

Java Ice Cream Fizz

> 2 tablespoons milk
> 4 teaspoons sugar
> 2 teaspoons instant coffee granules
>   Vanilla ice cream
> 1 7-ounce bottle ginger ale, chilled
>   (about 1 cup)

Combine milk, sugar, and instant coffee granules in a tall glass. Add a spoonful of vanilla ice cream; stir till ice cream melts. Add 2 scoops of vanilla ice cream; carefully pour in chilled ginger ale. Makes 1 serving.

Apricot-Tea Delight

Ginger ale adds sparkle—

> 2 cups hot tea
> 1 12-ounce can apricot nectar
> 1 cup orange juice
> ¼ cup sugar
> ¼ cup lemon juice
> 2 7-ounce bottles ginger ale, chilled
>   Ice cubes

Advance preparation: Combine hot tea, apricot nectar, orange juice, sugar, and lemon juice. Chill tea-apricot mixture thoroughly.
Before serving: Carefully pour in ginger ale. Serve over ice cubes. Makes 12 servings.

Frosty Orange Drink

Mix the drink quickly in the blender—

> ½ cup milk
> ½ cup cold water
> ½ of a 6-ounce can frozen orange juice
>   concentrate (⅓ cup)
> ½ teaspoon vanilla
> ¼ cup sugar
> 5 or 6 ice cubes

In blender container combine milk, water, orange juice concentrate, vanilla, sugar, and ice cubes. Cover and blend till smooth, about 30 seconds. Serve at once. Serves 2 or 3.

Cool Coffee Eggnog

> 4 cups milk
> 2 beaten egg yolks
> ¼ cup sugar
> 2 tablespoons instant coffee
>   granules
> 1 teaspoon vanilla
> ¼ teaspoon salt
>   • • •
> 2 egg whites
> 3 tablespoons sugar

Advance preparation: Stir milk into beaten egg yolks. Add the ¼ cup sugar, instant coffee granules, vanilla, and salt. Cook over medium heat, stirring constantly, till mixture coats a metal spoon. Chill mixture thoroughly.
Before serving: Beat egg whites till foamy. Gradually add the 3 tablespoons sugar, beating till soft peaks form. Add to coffee mixture and mix thoroughly. Makes 6 to 8 servings.

Coffee Especial

A perfect snack for chilly evenings—

> ¼ cup packed brown sugar
> 2 tablespoons instant coffee granules
>   Dash salt
> 4 cups milk

In saucepan combine brown sugar, coffee granules, and salt. Stir in milk. Heat through but do not boil. Serve in mugs. Makes 4 cups.

Purple Cows

Rich grape drink shown on page 32 —

¼ cup milk
2 tablespoons frozen grape juice
concentrate
1 tablespoon frozen lemonade
concentrate
1 pint vanilla ice cream
Frozen whipped dessert topping,
thawed (optional)
Mint leaves (optional)

In blender container combine milk, frozen juice concentrates, and ice cream. Cover and blend till smooth. Serve in tall glasses with straws. Garnish with whipped dessert topping and mint leaves, if desired. Serves 1 or 2.

Cran-Raspberry Float

Flavorful beverage shown on the cover —

1 pint raspberry sherbet
3 cups cranberry juice cocktail
1 12-ounce bottle lemon-lime
carbonated beverage, chilled
Mint sprigs *or* fresh or frozen
raspberries (optional)

Fill each of 4 tall glasses with spoonfuls of raspberry sherbet. Pour ¾ *cup* cranberry juice cocktail into *each* glass. Carefully fill with lemon-lime carbonated beverage; stir gently. Garnish with mint sprigs or fresh or frozen raspberries, if desired. Makes 4 servings.

Orange-Flavored Eggnog

1 pint vanilla ice cream
½ of a 6-ounce can frozen orange
juice concentrate, thawed (⅓ cup)
1 egg
2 cups milk
Ground nutmeg

In mixing bowl combine vanilla ice cream, orange juice concentrate, and egg; beat with electric or rotary beater. Gradually add milk, beating constantly. Pour into chilled mugs; sprinkle with ground nutmeg. Serves 6.

Apricot Shake

2 cups milk
1 21-ounce can apricot pie filling
1 quart vanilla ice cream

Pour *half* of the milk into blender container. Add *half* of the apricot pie filling; spoon in *half* of the ice cream. Cover; blend till ingredients are combined. Pour mixture into 3 tall glasses. Repeat with remaining milk, pie filling, and ice cream. Makes 6 servings.

Pink Peach Shake

1 cup milk
½ of a 6-ounce can frozen pink
lemonade concentrate, thawed
1 12-ounce package frozen peaches,
partially thawed
1 pint vanilla ice cream, softened

In blender container combine milk, lemonade concentrate, and peaches. Cover; blend till smooth. Add ice cream by spoonfuls; cover and blend till just smooth. Serves 3.

Rosy Nectarine Float

3 nectarines
2 pints pineapple sherbet,
slightly softened
1 6-ounce can frozen lemonade
concentrate
2½ cups water
4 cups cranberry juice cocktail,
chilled

Advance preparation: Chop *2* of the nectarines. Place the chopped nectarines and ½ *cup* of the sherbet in blender container. Cover and blend till smooth. Combine with the remaining sherbet; freeze firm. Stir lemonade concentrate with the water till dissolved; chill.
Before serving: Scoop sherbet mixture into tall glasses. Combine cranberry juice cocktail and chilled lemonade mixture; pour into glasses. Slice remaining nectarine; place 1 slice on rim of each glass. Garnish with fresh mint sprigs, if desired. Makes 8 to 10 servings.

Pineapple-Lime Float

1 12-ounce can pineapple juice,
   chilled (1½ cups)
1 cup water
½ of a 6-ounce can frozen limeade
   concentrate, thawed (⅓ cup)
1 quart lime sherbet
2 7-ounce bottles ginger ale, chilled

Combine pineapple juice, water, and limeade concentrate. Divide pineapple mixture among 6 tall glasses. Spoon *half* of the lime sherbet into the glasses; stir gently. Carefully pour chilled ginger ale into each glass. Top with scoops of remaining lime sherbet. Garnish with mint leaves, if desired. Makes 6 servings.

Mint-Chocolate Malted

½ cup semisweet chocolate pieces
4 cups milk
⅔ cup plain malted milk powder
1 teaspoon vanilla
   Several drops mint extract

Place chocolate pieces in saucepan; add *1 cup* of the milk. Heat and stir over low heat till chocolate pieces melt. Stir in remaining milk, malted milk powder, vanilla, and mint extract; heat through. Beat with rotary beater till frothy; pour into cups or mugs. Serves 6.

Instant Russian Tea Mix

½ cup orange-flavored breakfast
   drink powder
½ cup instant tea powder
¼ cup sugar
½ of a 3-ounce envelope presweetened
   lemonade mix (3 tablespoons)
¼ teaspoon ground cinnamon
⅛ teaspoon ground cloves

Measure all ingredients into a 1-quart screw-top jar. Shake gently to thoroughly combine.
   For hot tea: Measure 1 tablespoon mix into cup. Fill with boiling water.
   For iced tea: Measure 2 tablespoons mix into tall glass; add cold water and ice.

Cantaloupe-Orange Frost

¼ cup milk
¼ cup dairy sour cream
1 tablespoon sugar
½ ripe medium cantaloupe, peeled,
   seeded, and cut up (1¾ cups)
1 cup orange sherbet
   Cantaloupe balls (optional)

Advance preparation: Combine milk, dairy sour cream, and sugar in blender container. Add cantaloupe pieces. Cover and blend on high speed for 10 seconds. Chill well.
Before serving: Add sherbet by spoonfuls; cover and blend till smooth, about 10 seconds. Pour into 4 chilled glasses. Garnish with cantaloupe balls, if desired. Makes 4 servings.

A refreshing nectarine-pineapple sherbet mixture teams up with a brightly colored cranberry juice and lemonade mixture in *Rosy Nectarine Float.*

Snacks to Fit a Diet

Italian-Style Nibble Mix

64 calories per ½-cup serving —

¼ cup unpopped popcorn
2 cups bite-size shredded wheat
squares
2 cups puffed oat cereal
2 tablespoons butter or margarine,
melted
¼ cup grated Parmesan cheese
1 tablespoon Italian salad
dressing mix

Pop the popcorn in a heavy skillet or saucepan over medium-high heat, *using no oil in the pan.* Be sure to cover the skillet and shake the pan constantly until all the corn is popped. In 13x9x2-inch baking pan combine the popped corn, wheat squares, and puffed oat cereal. Heat in 300° oven till warm, about 5 minutes. Remove from oven. Drizzle melted butter or margarine over popcorn-cereal mixture. Combine Parmesan cheese and salad dressing mix; sprinkle over corn. Stir well. Makes 9 cups.

Stuffed Cherry Tomatoes

13 calories per snack —

24 cherry tomatoes
1 3¼-ounce can tuna (water pack)
2 tablespoons plain yogurt
1 teaspoon snipped chives
½ teaspoon prepared mustard
¼ teaspoon salt

Advance preparation: Cut small slice off bottoms of cherry tomatoes so they will sit flat. Cut thin slice from tops of tomatoes. With small melon baller or spoon carefully scoop out centers; discard. Sprinkle insides with salt and pepper. Invert and chill. Drain tuna thoroughly. Combine tuna, yogurt, chives, prepared mustard, and the ¼ teaspoon salt. Chill.
Before serving: Fill tomatoes with tuna mixture, using 1 to 1½ teaspoons for each tomato. Garnish with parsley, if desired. Makes 24.

Dilled Cauliflowerets

39 calories per ½-cup serving —

1 medium head cauliflower,
broken into flowerets
(4 cups)
¾ cup low-calorie Italian
salad dressing
1 tablespoon chopped canned pimiento
1 tablespoon finely chopped onion
½ teaspoon dried dillweed

Advance preparation: Cook cauliflowerets, covered, in small amount of boiling salted water just till crisp-tender, about 10 minutes. Drain; place in shallow dish. Combine Italian salad dressing, pimiento, onion, and dried dillweed; pour over warm cauliflowerets. Cover; marinate in refrigerator several hours or overnight, stirring occasionally.
Before serving: Drain cauliflowerets. Serve with wooden picks. Makes 4 cups.

Apricot-Orange Nog

54 calories per ½-cup serving —

1 cup orange juice, chilled
½ cup skim milk
¼ teaspoon vanilla
1 16-ounce can apricot halves (juice
pack), chilled
1 ripe medium banana, cut up

In blender container combine chilled orange juice, skim milk, vanilla, undrained apricot halves, and cut-up ripe banana. Cover and blend till smooth. Pour mixture into small juice glasses. Serve immediately. Serves 8.

Calorie-reduced snacks

Spice up your diet with tantalizing *Italian-Style Nibble Mix, Stuffed Cherry Tomatoes, Dilled Cauliflowerets,* or thick *Apricot-Orange Nog.*

Spicy Pineapple Chunks

6 calories per snack —

1 20-ounce can pineapple chunks
(juice pack)
1 tablespoon sugar
1 tablespoon vinegar
6 inches stick cinnamon
6 whole cloves

Advance preparation: Drain pineapple, reserving juice; set pineapple aside. In small saucepan combine reserved juice, sugar, vinegar, stick cinnamon, and whole cloves. Simmer mixture, uncovered, for 5 minutes. Add pineapple chunks; heat through. Cool. Store in covered container in refrigerator at least 48 hours. Serve on wooden picks. Makes 60.

Zippy Tomato Cooler

33 calories per serving —

½ medium cucumber
1 whole canned green chili pepper
1 18-ounce can tomato juice, chilled
1 cup buttermilk
1 teaspoon Worcestershire sauce
1 teaspoon lemon juice
Ice cubes

Peel cucumber; halve lengthwise and remove seeds. Cut in pieces. Drain and seed chili pepper. In blender container combine tomato juice, buttermilk, Worcestershire, lemon juice, cucumber, and pepper. Cover; blend till cucumber is pureed. Serve over ice. If desired, serve with cucumber stick stirrers. Serves 6.

Cottage and Blue Cheese Dip

20 calories per tablespoon —

Place one 12-ounce carton cream-style cottage cheese, ¼ cup crumbled blue cheese, 2 tablespoons skim milk, 1 teaspoon lemon juice, and 1 small clove garlic in blender container. Cover; blend till smooth, stopping occasionally to scrape down sides. Turn into serving bowl. Sprinkle with paprika. Serve with vegetable dippers (see tip, page 36). Makes 1½ cups dip.

Vegetable-Beef Broth

28 calories per ½-cup serving —

Heat one 12-ounce can vegetable juice cocktail, one 10½-ounce can condensed beef broth, and ½ cup water. Serve in mugs. Serves 6.

Calorie-trimming snack tips

• Reserve a part of your meal, such as the salad or dessert course, for an afternoon or late-evening snack.
• When counting calories, remember to include your calorie intake from snacks.
• Snacks don't have to be just empty calories. Use a snack to fulfill part of your nutritional needs. For example, a milk-based beverage supplies calcium, protein, and vitamins A and D, a meat sandwich contributes protein, and fresh fruits and vegetables provide vitamins A and C, minerals, and roughage.
• Don't go overboard eating snack foods. Keep the serving portions small.
• Snack on dill pickles, celery, cucumber, green pepper, radishes, bouillon, and cauliflower often. These foods can be eaten in unlimited quantities.
• Fresh fruits and vegetables are low in calories and make excellent snacks.
• Canned fruits packed in water, juice, or slightly sweetened syrup are lower in calories than syrup-pack fruits. Some of the calories in syrup-pack fruits can be eliminated by rinsing the fruit with water.
• Make sandwiches with thin-sliced bread. Or, serve open-face sandwiches.
• Save calories by flavoring yogurt yourself. Just add crushed fruit and a bit of sugar to plain yogurt.
• Use skim milk or reconstituted nonfat dry milk rather than whole milk when preparing snacks and beverages.
• Serve low-calorie dippers such as vegetables, fruits, and seafood with low-calorie dips and spreads.
• Use low-calorie carbonated beverages in fruit drinks and punches.

Creamy Apricot Dip

17 calories per tablespoon —

½ of a 12-ounce can apricot
    nectar (¾ cup)
2 teaspoons cornstarch
1 tablespoon honey
½ teaspoon shredded orange peel
½ cup plain yogurt
⅓ cup frozen whipped dessert topping,
    thawed
Fruit dippers (see tip, page 36)

Advance preparation: In saucepan blend nectar and cornstarch. Stir in honey and orange peel. Cook and stir over medium heat till thickened and bubbly. Reduce heat; cook and stir 1 minute longer. Remove from heat; cool. Blend in yogurt and dessert topping. Chill. Serve with fruit dippers. Makes 1⅓ cups dip.

Yogurt-Cucumber Dip

9 calories per tablespoon —

1 8-ounce carton plain yogurt
¼ cup well-drained, finely shredded
    cucumber
1 tablespoon snipped parsley
½ teaspoon grated onion
¼ teaspoon garlic salt
¼ teaspoon Worcestershire sauce
Vegetable dippers (see tip, page 36)

Stir together plain yogurt, shredded cucumber, snipped parsley, grated onion, garlic salt, and Worcestershire sauce. Serve with crisp vegetable dippers. Makes 1¼ cups dip.

Sugared Melon Cup

45 calories per serving —

¾ cup diced fresh pineapple
¾ cup unsweetened fresh raspberries
1 small cantaloupe, chilled and cut
    in 6 wedges
2 tablespoons sifted powdered sugar

Combine pineapple and raspberries; fill melon cavities with fruits. Top *each* wedge with *1 teaspoon* powdered sugar. Serves 6.

Shrimp Fondue

109 calories per serving —

1 pound fresh or frozen shelled shrimp
½ cup low-calorie Thousand Island
    salad dressing
2 teaspoons lemon juice
1 teaspoon snipped chives
4 teaspoons instant chicken bouillon
    granules
1 tablespoon lemon juice
1 teaspoon grated onion

Thaw frozen shrimp. Combine dressing, 2 teaspoons lemon juice, and chives. In metal fondue cooker combine bouillon granules, 1 tablespoon lemon juice, onion, and 3 cups water. Heat to boiling over range. Transfer cooker to fondue burner. Have shrimp at room temperature in serving container. Spear shrimp with fondue fork. Cook in hot broth till done. Dip in dressing mixture. Serves 6.

Cheeseburger Snacks

32 calories per snack —

Cut 2 ounces sharp American cheese into 24 small cubes. Combine 1 egg, ¾ cup soft bread crumbs, 2 tablespoons chopped green onion, 1 tablespoon water, ½ teaspoon Worcestershire sauce, ¼ teaspoon garlic salt, and dash pepper. Mix in ½ pound lean ground beef. Form into 24 meatballs, shaping each around cheese cube. Place on foil-lined 15½x10½x1-inch baking pan. Bake at 375° for 12 to 15 minutes. Makes 24 snacks.

Chilies-Cheese Stuffed Eggs

53 calories per egg half —

6 hard-cooked eggs
¼ cup process cheese spread
2 tablespoons chopped canned green
    chili peppers
Paprika

Advance preparation: Halve eggs lengthwise. Remove yolks; mash. Blend yolks with cheese spread, peppers, and dash salt. Refill whites; sprinkle with paprika. Chill. Makes 12.

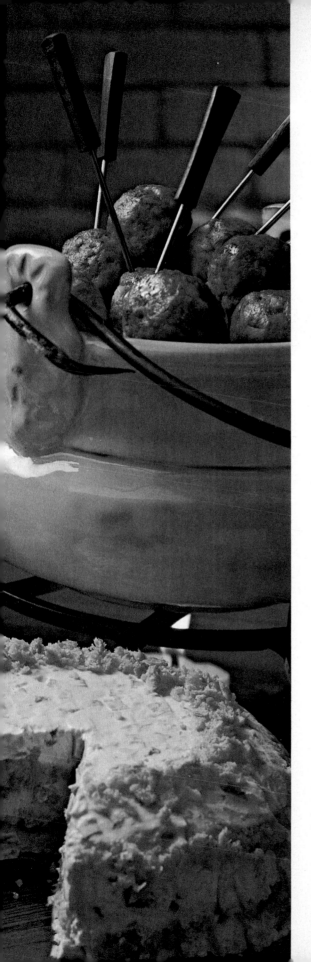

Appetizer Assortment

When planning the menu for your next party, include one or more taste-tempting appetizers to add a special flair.

For a cocktail party, select a decorative cheese ball or cocktail meatballs. Then, add a sparkling punch to go with the appetizers. If you're giving a tea, tiny sandwiches are ideal. For a dinner party, begin with a first-course fruit cup or seafood cocktail.

Diet-conscious guests will appreciate being served a low-calorie appetizer. You'll discover several tantalizing calorie-reduced recipes in this section. You'll also find over 20 delectable cost-cutting recipes to help you entertain elegantly on a budget.

And don't forget to consult the Party Menus chart for ideas. It can help make party-giving easy and enjoyable.

Treat your guests to Mexican-flavored *Notches*, *Clam and Avocado Dip, Chestnut Meatballs, Appetizer Cheesecake*, low-calorie *Shrimp-Cucumber Dip*, and radish-garnished *Anchovy-Cheese Ball*. (See index for page numbers.)

Definitely Fancy

Mosaic Sandwiches

    1 tablespoon milk
    1 teaspoon Worcestershire sauce
    1 3-ounce package cream cheese,
        softened
    4 slices bacon, crisp-cooked,
        drained, and crumbled
      White sandwich bread
      Whole wheat sandwich bread

Blend milk and Worcestershire into cream cheese. Fold in bacon. With cookie cutter cut an equal amount of white and whole wheat bread into rectangles or bell shapes. Spread half of the cutouts (use an equal number of white and whole wheat) with cheese mixture. With small hors d'oeuvres cutters, cut shapes from centers of remaining bread cutouts; fit together contrasting bread cutouts. (Use whole wheat shapes over white bread sandwiches and vice versa.) If desired, garnish with snipped parsley or chopped canned pimiento.

Ham-Cheese Checkerboards

    1 unsliced loaf white sandwich bread
    1 unsliced loaf whole wheat sandwich
        bread
      Cheese Butter
      Ham Filling

Remove crusts from bread. From each loaf cut 6 lengthwise slices, ½ inch thick. Following the Checkerboard directions on page 71, use Cheese Butter and Ham Filling to put bread together. (For the larger checkerboards shown at right, stack six slices in each loaf.) Chill and cut as directed.

  Cheese Butter: Combine one 5-ounce jar sharp process cheese spread and ½ cup butter or margarine, softened.

  Ham Filling: Combine one 8-ounce package cream cheese, softened; one 4½-ounce can deviled ham; 1 tablespoon catsup; and 1 to 2 teaspoons finely chopped onion.

Egg Salad Miniatures

    4 hard-cooked eggs, chopped
    ⅓ cup chopped pimiento-
        stuffed green olives
    2 tablespoons finely chopped green
        onion
    ¼ cup mayonnaise or salad dressing
    2 teaspoons prepared mustard
      White sandwich bread

Combine eggs, olives, and onion; blend in mayonnaise and mustard. Cut bread with small crescent-shaped cutter. Spread with egg mixture. If desired, garnish with shapes cut from jellied cranberry sauce. *Or,* spread filling on tiny bread rounds. If desired, garnish bread rounds with sliced pimiento-stuffed green olives, halved. Makes 1½ cups filling.

Tuna Roll-Ups

Trim crusts from 1 unsliced loaf white sandwich bread. Cut bread into 8 lengthwise slices about ¼ inch thick. Roll bread lightly with a rolling pin. Spread bread with softened butter or margarine. Spread each slice with about ¼ cup Tuna-Pimiento Filling. Place 5 very thin strips green pepper crosswise, equal distance apart, atop filling *on each bread slice.* Roll up jelly-roll fashion, beginning at narrow end. Wrap; chill thoroughly. Slice crosswise into ⅜-inch-thick slices. Makes 40.

  Tuna-Pimiento Filling: Drain and flake two 6½- or 7-ounce cans tuna. Mix tuna, ⅔ cup mayonnaise, 2 tablespoons mashed canned pimiento, and 1 tablespoon prepared mustard.

Assortment of elegant appetizers

Serve guests *Hearts of Palm Relish, Shrimp-Cucumber Rounds, Tuna Roll-Ups, Egg Salad Miniatures, Mosaic Sandwiches, Ham-Cheese Checkerboards, Watercress Pinwheels,* and *Appetizer Pies.* (See the index for recipe page numbers.)

Shrimp Canapés

1 cup chopped cooked shrimp
½ cup chopped cucumber
1 teaspoon finely chopped onion
⅛ teaspoon salt
¼ cup mayonnaise or salad dressing
2 teaspoons lemon juice
8 slices white sandwich bread

Combine first 4 ingredients; blend in mayonnaise and lemon juice. Chill. Toast bread; trim crusts. Spread shrimp mixture on toast. Cut each toast slice into 4 triangles. Garnish with cucumber twist, if desired. Makes 32.

Watercress Pinwheels

Tiny appetizer rounds shown on page 69 —

1 unsliced loaf white sandwich bread
1 cup chopped watercress
2 3-ounce packages cream cheese, softened

Remove crusts from bread. Slice bread lengthwise in slices ⅜ inch thick. Combine watercress, cheese, and dash salt. Spread about ¼ cup cheese mixture on each bread slice. Roll up, starting at narrow end. Wrap in foil; chill well. Slice ⅜ inch thick. Makes about 24.

Shrimp-Cucumber Rounds

These petite sandwiches are shown on page 69 —

1 3-ounce package cream cheese, softened
2 tablespoons mayonnaise
1 tablespoon catsup
1 teaspoon prepared mustard
    Dash garlic powder
1 cup chopped cooked shrimp
¼ cup finely chopped cucumber
1 teaspoon finely chopped onion
    Party rye bread

Blend together the cheese and mayonnaise; stir in catsup, mustard, and garlic powder. Stir in shrimp, cucumber, and onion. Spread over rye bread rounds. Garnish with additional shrimp and cucumber, if desired. Makes 20.

Frosted Ribbon Loaf

1 unsliced loaf white sandwich bread
    Butter or margarine, softened
    Ham Salad Filling
1 tomato, peeled and thinly sliced
    Egg Salad Filling
4 3-ounce packages cream cheese, softened
⅓ cup milk
    Snipped chives

Trim crusts from bread; slice bread lengthwise into 4 slices. Spread with butter. Spread one bread slice with Ham Salad Filling, arrange tomato on another bread slice, and spread Egg Salad Filling on a third bread slice. Assemble loaf, using 2 spatulas to support layers. Top with remaining bread slice. Wrap; chill. At serving time, beat cream cheese with milk till fluffy. Frost loaf with cheese mixture. Sprinkle with chives. Slice thinly to serve. Serves 10.

Ham Salad Filling: In mixing bowl combine 1 cup ground fully cooked ham, ⅓ cup finely chopped celery, ¼ cup mayonnaise or salad dressing, 2 tablespoons drained sweet pickle relish, and ½ teaspoon prepared horseradish.

Egg Salad Filling: Combine 4 hard-cooked eggs, chopped; ⅓ cup chopped pimiento-stuffed green olives; ¼ cup mayonnaise; 2 tablespoons finely chopped green onion; and 2 teaspoons prepared mustard.

Chopped Liver

½ pound chicken livers *or* goose livers
½ cup chopped onion
2 tablespoons chicken fat *or* cooking oil
2 hard-cooked eggs
½ teaspoon salt
    Lettuce
    Assorted crackers

Cook livers and onion in fat till livers are no longer pink. Put livers, onion, and egg whites through fine blade of food chopper. Add salt and ⅛ teaspoon pepper; mix well. Chill. To serve, mound on lettuce-lined plate. Sieve egg yolks; sprinkle atop liver mixture. Serve with crackers. Makes 1¾ cups spread.

Cornucopias: With a serrated knife, trim crusts from bread slices (stack 3 slices for easier trimming). Spread with softened cheese spread. Carefully roll into cornucopias as shown. Trim with petals made from ripe olives. Place on flat pan, seam side down, and chill till serving time.

Fold-Ups: With a serrated knife, trim crusts from bread slices (stack 3 slices for easier trimming). Spread with softened cheese spread. Bring two opposite corners together at center. Secure with wooden pick; garnish with watercress.

Pinwheels: Have bakery trim crusts from 1 loaf unsliced sandwich bread and cut loaf *lengthwise* in slices ¼ inch thick. (Or, at home, use an electric knife for ease in slicing bread.) Spread each bread slice with softened cheese spread, parsley butter (combine butter with snipped parsley), or a meat or seafood salad mixture (ham, chicken, or tuna). For pretty center, line up a row of pimiento-stuffed green olives, crosswise, near end of each slice as shown. Starting at short end, roll up bread jelly-roll fashion; wrap in foil or clear plastic wrap. Chill, seam side down. Before serving, place roll, seam side down, on cutting board. Using sharp knife, carefully cut roll crosswise into ⅜-inch slices.

Jigsaws: Using half white and half whole wheat bread, cut bread slices into 2-inch rounds. For sandwich bottoms, spread *half* the rounds of each color with seafood salad mixture or cheese spread. Make tops by cutting circles from remaining rounds with hole of doughnut cutter. Fit tiny whole wheat circles into white rings and vice versa. Assemble sandwiches by placing tops and bottoms together. *Or,* cut bread rounds into strips or quarters; arrange atop salad mixture, alternating colors. Another time, use tiny sandwich or cookie cutters for a variety of different shapes.

Checkerboards: Have bakery trim the crusts from two unsliced loaves sandwich bread—one white and one whole wheat. From *each* loaf, cut six *lengthwise* slices about ½ inch thick. Use your favorite filling or spread to put four slices bread together, alternating white and whole wheat. Repeat to make a total of three loaves. Wrap in foil or clear plastic wrap; chill. Slice each loaf into six *lengthwise* slices as shown. Put four of these slices together with additional filling, alternating colors to make checkerboard loaf (shown at left). Repeat to make a total of four loaves. (There will be two slices remaining; cut each of these crosswise into 4 or 5 ribbon sandwiches.) Wrap loaves and chill once more; cut each loaf *crosswise* in about ½-inch slices to make checkerboard sandwiches.

Hearts of Palm Relish

Colorful marinated relish shown on page 69 —

¼ cup salad oil
1 tablespoon finely chopped onion
1 tablespoon snipped parsley
1 tablespoon vinegar
1 teaspoon lemon juice
¼ teaspoon salt
⅛ teaspoon dry mustard
1 hard-cooked egg, finely chopped
1 tablespoon chopped canned pimiento
1 14-ounce can hearts of palm,
   chilled
Lettuce

In screw-top jar combine oil, onion, parsley, vinegar, lemon juice, salt, and dry mustard. Cover; shake vigorously to blend. Add egg and pimiento; stir well. Drain hearts of palm and cut in strips. Line relish dish with lettuce; arrange hearts of palm on lettuce. Pour oil mixture over. Makes about 1½ cups relish.

Appetizer Pies

Impressive appetizer pictured on page 69 —

1 hard-cooked egg
1 4½-ounce can deviled ham
1 teaspoon prepared horseradish
1 teaspoon prepared mustard
1 6- or 7-inch unsliced round loaf
   rye bread
1 tablespoon mayonnaise or salad
   dressing
Dash dried dillweed
1 5-ounce jar process cheese spread
2 medium cucumbers, scored and sliced
1 2-ounce jar red caviar

Separate egg yolk and white; chop egg white finely. Sieve egg yolk; set aside. Combine deviled ham, horseradish, and mustard. Cut four ½-inch-thick crosswise slices from center of rye loaf. (Use remaining bread elsewhere.) Combine mayonnaise and dillweed; spread over each bread slice. Spread ham filling in center; ring with cheese spread. Halve cucumber slices; arrange atop cheese, overlapping edges. Add a ring of caviar. Fill center with chopped egg white and sieved yolk. Makes 4.

Pickled Artichokes and Mushrooms

⅓ cup vinegar
⅓ cup salad oil
2 tablespoons sugar
2 tablespoons snipped parsley
1½ teaspoons salt
1 clove garlic, crushed
¼ teaspoon whole black pepper
Dash bottled hot pepper sauce
1 14-ounce can artichoke hearts
1 cup sliced fresh mushrooms

Combine vinegar, oil, sugar, parsley, salt, garlic, pepper, hot pepper sauce, and ⅓ cup water. Drain artichokes. In shallow dish or deep, narrow glass jar pour vinegar mixture over artichokes and mushrooms. Cover; chill 8 hours or overnight, stirring occasionally. Drain to serve. Makes about 2½ cups.

Baked Liver Pâté

1 pound chicken livers
¼ cup chopped onion
1 bay leaf
1¼ cups milk
1 egg
2 tablespoons fine dry bread crumbs
1 tablespoon cornstarch
1 teaspoon salt
⅛ teaspoon pepper
2 3-ounce packages cream cheese,
   softened
Assorted crackers

Simmer chicken livers, onion, and bay leaf, covered, in small amount of water for 8 to 10 minutes; remove bay leaf. Drain; cool slightly. In blender container place ½ cup of the milk and the liver mixture. Cover; blend on medium speed till smooth. Add the remaining milk, egg, crumbs, cornstarch, salt, and pepper. Cover; blend till combined. Pour into 4-cup ovenproof mold. Set in shallow baking pan; pour hot water around mold in pan to depth of ½ inch. Bake at 325° till knife inserted off-center comes out clean, 1 to 1¼ hours. Chill. Unmold onto serving plate. Using star tip on pastry tube, pipe cream cheese atop and around edges of pâté. Serve with crackers.

Chicken Puffs

    2 cups finely chopped cooked chicken
    ⅓ cup mayonnaise or salad dressing
    ¼ cup finely chopped celery
    2 tablespoons chopped canned pimiento
    2 tablespoons dry white wine *or* water
    ¼ teaspoon salt
      Dash pepper
    ⅔ cup water
    1 stick piecrust mix
    2 eggs

In mixing bowl combine chicken, mayonnaise, celery, pimiento, wine, salt, and pepper. Cover; chill. In small saucepan heat ⅔ cup water to boiling. Crumble piecrust mix. Add to water; stir vigorously over low heat till pastry forms a ball and pulls away from sides of pan. Cook and stir 1 minute longer. Add eggs and beat on low speed of electric mixer for 2 minutes. Drop dough by rounded teaspoons onto *ungreased* baking sheet. Bake at 425° till puffed, golden, and dry, 20 to 25 minutes. Cool slowly on rack away from draft. Split puffs; remove inside webbing, if desired. Just before serving, fill with chicken mixture. Makes 42.

Chicken Salad Tarts

    1 stick piecrust mix
    2 tablespoons sesame seed, toasted
    ½ cup mayonnaise or salad dressing
    ½ cup dairy sour cream
    2 tablespoons finely chopped chutney
    ½ teaspoon curry powder
    2 cups chopped cooked chicken
  1½ cups diced fresh pineapple
    1 cup chopped celery
    ¼ cup slivered almonds, toasted

Prepare and roll out piecrust mix according to package directions; sprinkle with sesame seed. Fold up and reroll till ⅛ inch thick. Cut and fit pastry into 6 tart pans; flute edges. Prick bottoms and sides well with fork. Bake according to piecrust mix package directions; cool. Combine mayonnaise, sour cream, chutney, and curry powder. Add chicken, pineapple, celery, and almonds. Toss lightly. Spoon into tart shells. Makes 6 servings.

Chicken Liver-Pimiento Rolls

    ½ pound chicken livers, chopped
    1 tablespoon butter or margarine
          • • •
    2 hard-cooked eggs, chopped
    ¼ cup chopped canned pimiento
    ¼ cup mayonnaise or salad dressing
    1 teaspoon finely chopped onion
    1 teaspoon prepared mustard
    ¼ teaspoon salt
      Dash Worcestershire sauce
  20 tiny party rolls

Cook chicken livers in butter till livers just begin to loose pink color, about 5 minutes. Stir in eggs, pimiento, mayonnaise, onion, mustard, salt, and Worcestershire sauce. Split rolls. Spread bottom half of each party roll with about 1 tablespoon chicken liver mixture; replace top. Makes 20 small sandwiches.

Cheese Boreck

    1 16-ounce package frozen fillo dough
      (twenty 16x12-inch sheets)
    2 cups shredded Muenster cheese
      (8 ounces)
    2 3-ounce packages cream cheese,
      softened
    ¼ cup cream-style cottage cheese
    1 egg
    ½ teaspoon instant minced onion
    ¾ cup butter or margarine, melted

Thaw frozen fillo dough. Combine Muenster cheese, cream cheese, cottage cheese, egg, and instant minced onion. Beat smooth. Stack together two sheets fillo dough. Brush top with about *1 tablespoon* of the melted butter. Cut dough into eight 12x2-inch strips. Place 2 teaspoons cheese mixture in corner at end of one strip. Pick up adjacent corner; fold over filling, forming a triangle. Continue folding in triangle form to end of strip. Trim any ragged edges. Repeat with remaining dough, butter, and cheese filling to make eight appetizers from each two sheets of dough. Cover; chill. Place appetizers, folded side down, on *ungreased* baking sheets. Bake at 400° about 20 minutes. Makes 80 appetizers.

Flaming Greek Cheese

    4 ounces Kasseri cheese *or* mozzarella
        cheese, cut in ¼-inch-thick slices
    2 tablespoons Metaxa *or* another brandy
    ½ lemon
        Thinly sliced French bread, toasted

Place cheese on sizzle platter, oven-going skillet, or pie plate. Broil till cheese is just soft and the surface bubbles slightly, about 7 minutes. Warm Metaxa; flame and pour over cheese. Squeeze lemon over cheese. Spread cheese on toasted bread. Makes 4 servings.

Dill-Bread Stuffed Mushrooms

    24 large fresh mushrooms
     2 tablespoons sliced green onion with
        tops
     2 tablespoons butter or margarine
     ¼ cup fine dry bread crumbs
     ½ teaspoon dried dillweed
     ⅛ teaspoon salt
     ⅛ teaspoon Worcestershire sauce

Remove stems from mushrooms; chop stems. Cook stems and onion in butter till tender. Remove from heat. Stir in remaining ingredients; fill mushroom crowns. Bake on greased baking sheet at 425° for 6 to 8 minutes. Makes 24.

To assemble *Chinese Egg Rolls,* fold one edge of the thin pancake over the pork and shrimp filling. Fold in the two sides, then roll up and press to seal.

Chinese Egg Rolls

    ½ cup bean sprouts, drained
    ½ cup finely chopped cooked pork
    ¼ cup finely chopped cooked shrimp
    ¼ cup finely chopped celery
    ¼ cup water chestnuts, drained and
        finely chopped
    1 tablespoon finely chopped onion
    1 slightly beaten egg
    1 tablespoon cooking oil
    1 teaspoon soy sauce
    ½ teaspoon sugar
    ¼ teaspoon salt
        • • •
    1⅓ cups all-purpose flour
    ⅔ cup cornstarch
    1 teaspoon salt
    2 beaten eggs
    1½ cups water
        Cooking oil

In mixing bowl combine bean sprouts, pork, shrimp, celery, water chestnuts, onion, 1 slightly beaten egg, 1 tablespoon cooking oil, soy, sugar, and ¼ teaspoon salt. Cover; chill.

In mixing bowl stir flour, cornstarch, and 1 teaspoon salt together thoroughly. Combine the 2 beaten eggs and the water; gradually blend into dry ingredients. Beat smooth with rotary beater. Lightly grease a 6-inch heavy skillet; heat. Set aside ½ cup of the batter for sealing edges of egg rolls. Pour about 2 tablespoons of the remaining batter into skillet, lifting and tipping skillet till batter evenly covers bottom. Cook over medium heat till top looks dry and edges begin to curl. Do not turn. Place on paper toweling. Repeat with remaining batter, greasing pan occasionally.

To assemble egg rolls, place about 1 tablespoon chilled pork filling near edge of each pancake. Brush edges with some of the reserved batter. Fold edge nearest filling up and over filling; fold in the two sides. Roll up, pressing gently to seal. (If desired, refrigerate uncooked egg rolls till ready to fry.) Pour cooking oil into deep skillet to depth of 1½ inches. Heat to 375°. Fry a few egg rolls at a time, about 6 minutes. Drain on paper toweling. Repeat till all egg rolls are cooked. Serve with bottled hot mustard and sweet-sour sauces, if desired. Makes 18 egg rolls.

Teriyaki Appetizer Ribs

        4 pounds meaty pork spareribs, sawed
            in half crosswise
    ½ cup soy sauce
    ¼ cup honey
    2 tablespoons lemon juice
    1 tablespoon packed brown sugar
    1 clove garlic, minced
    ½ teaspoon ground ginger
    ¼ teaspoon pepper

Cut meat into 2-rib portions. Cover ribs with boiling salted water; cover pan and simmer till ribs are tender, 30 to 45 minutes. Drain. Combine remaining ingredients. Place ribs in shallow roasting pan. Pour sauce over ribs. Bake at 350° about 20 minutes, basting occasionally. Makes about 26 appetizers.

Chestnut Meatballs

    2 cups soft bread crumbs (2½ slices)
    ½ cup milk
    1 tablespoon soy sauce
    ½ teaspoon garlic salt
    ¼ teaspoon onion powder
    ½ pound ground beef
    ½ pound bulk pork sausage
    1 5-ounce can water chestnuts, drained
        and finely chopped

Combine crumbs, milk, soy, garlic salt, and onion powder. Add beef, sausage, and water chestnuts; mix well. Form into 1-inch balls. Bake on 15½x10½x1-inch baking pan at 350° for 18 to 20 minutes. Makes about 60.

Miniature Sesame Drumsticks

Cut 3 pounds chicken wings in pieces and use the meatier "drumstick" piece for appetizers. (Use remaining wing pieces for soups.) Combine ¼ cup finely crushed rich round crackers; ¼ cup sesame seed, toasted; 1 teaspoon paprika; and ¾ teaspoon salt. Brush meatier end of "drumsticks" with ¼ cup melted butter. Roll in cracker mixture. Place in large, shallow baking pan (don't crowd). Bake at 375° for 40 to 45 minutes. Makes 16 to 18 appetizers.

Piroshki

    ½ pound lean ground beef
    ½ cup finely chopped onion
    1 hard-cooked egg, chopped
    ½ teaspoon salt
        Dash pepper
    ½ of an 8-ounce package cream cheese
    ½ cup butter or margarine
    1¾ cups all-purpose flour

In small skillet cook beef and onion till meat is browned and onion is tender. Add chopped egg, salt, and pepper. In mixing bowl cut cream cheese and butter or margarine into flour till mixture resembles fine crumbs. Press mixture into a ball. Divide in half; roll one half to ⅛-inch thickness. Cut into 2¾-inch rounds. Place about 1 teaspoon meat mixture on each round; moisten edges with water and fold over. Press to seal with floured tines of fork. Repeat cutting and filling with remaining dough and meat mixture. Place on *ungreased* baking sheet. Bake at 400° till golden brown, 12 to 15 minutes. Makes about 36.

Broiled Scallop Puffs

    ¾ pound fresh or frozen scallops
    ½ teaspoon salt
    ¼ cup mayonnaise or salad dressing
    1 tablespoon sweet pickle relish
    1½ teaspoons lemon juice
    1 teaspoon snipped parsley
    ¼ teaspoon Worcestershire sauce
        Dash salt
        Dash pepper
    1 stiffly beaten egg white

Thaw frozen scallops. In saucepan cover scallops with water; add the ½ teaspoon salt. Cover saucepan and simmer about 10 minutes. Drain and cool. Cut scallops in half. Combine mayonnaise, pickle relish, lemon juice, parsley, Worcestershire sauce, dash salt, and pepper. Fold in stiffly beaten egg white. Place scallop halves on baking sheet or in a shallow pan. Top each with a little of the egg white mixture. Broil 3 to 4 inches from heat till golden brown, about 3 minutes. Serve immediately. Makes about 24 appetizers.

Appetizers on the Double

Salmon-Cucumber Appetizers

1 7¾-ounce can salmon, drained, bones
    and skin removed, and flaked
1 3-ounce package cream cheese,
    softened
1 tablespoon lemon juice
¼ teaspoon salt
¼ teaspoon dried dillweed
2 small cucumbers
    Canned pimiento

Blend together salmon, cream cheese, lemon juice, salt, dillweed, and dash pepper. Slice cucumbers ¼ inch thick. Place about 1 teaspoon salmon mixture on each cucumber slice. Garnish with small pieces of pimiento. Cover; chill till ready to serve. Makes about 48.

Turkey-Swiss Sandwiches

⅓ cup mayonnaise or salad
    dressing
1 teaspoon prepared mustard
1 5-ounce can boned turkey or chicken,
    drained and chopped
½ cup shredded Swiss cheese (2 ounces)
    Milk
12 slices raisin bread
    Butter or margarine, softened

Combine mayonnaise and mustard. Stir in turkey and cheese. Blend in a little milk, if necessary, to make of spreading consistency. Trim crusts from bread (stack 3 slices for easier trimming). Spread bread with butter. Spread half the slices with turkey mixture; top with remaining bread. Cut into thirds. Makes 18.

To highlight any occasion

← Prepare attractive *Olive Roll-Ups,* cool and crisp *Salmon-Cucumber Appetizers,* and *Garlic-Buttered Shrimp* (see recipe, page 81) in a jiffy.

Sour Cream-Salmon Spread

1 16-ounce can salmon, chilled
2 tablespoons lemon juice
    Dash freshly ground pepper
    Dash Worcestershire sauce
1 cup dairy sour cream
2 tablespoons finely chopped onion
1 tablespoon drained capers
    Snipped chives *or* capers, drained
    (optional)
    Melba toast rounds

Drain salmon; break up with a fork, removing bones and skin. Sprinkle salmon with lemon juice, pepper, and Worcestershire sauce, tossing to distribute. Arrange down center of small platter. Combine sour cream, onion, and the 1 tablespoon capers. Spoon over salmon. Garnish with snipped chives or additional capers, if desired. Serve with melba toast rounds. Makes about 2½ cups spread.

Olive Roll-Ups

Spread *a generous ½ tablespoon* whipped cream cheese on *each* of 4 slices boiled ham. Cut each slice into 6 strips. Wrap strips around 24 small pimiento-stuffed green olives. If desired, secure with cocktail picks. Makes 24.

Cranberry-Yogurt Dip

1 8-ounce carton plain yogurt (1 cup)
1 cup cranberry-orange relish
2 tablespoons sugar
⅛ teaspoon ground cinnamon
⅛ teaspoon ground nutmeg
    Cooked chicken, turkey, or ham cut
    in bite-size cubes

Combine plain yogurt, cranberry-orange relish, sugar, cinnamon, and nutmeg. Chill till ready to serve. Serve dip with chicken, turkey, or ham cubes. Makes about 2 cups dip.

Cream Cheese-Bacon Sandwiches

1 3-ounce package cream cheese,
   softened
4 slices bacon, crisp-cooked, drained,
   and crumbled
1 tablespoon milk
1 teaspoon prepared horseradish
½ teaspoon Worcestershire sauce
7 slices firm-textured whole wheat
   bread
   Canned pimiento strips, green pepper
   strips, parsley, and sliced
   pimiento-stuffed green olives

Combine cream cheese, bacon, milk, horse-radish, and Worcestershire; blend well. Using a cookie or hors d'oeuvre cutter, cut shapes from bread. Spread bread with cheese mixture. Decorate each sandwich with pimiento, green pepper, parsley, or olive. Makes 20.

Horseradish-Cream Cheese Canapés

1 3-ounce package cream cheese,
   softened
2 tablespoons dairy sour cream
1 tablespoon snipped parsley
½ teaspoon grated fresh horseradish
   Party rye bread, toasted

In a bowl beat together cream cheese and sour cream. Stir in parsley and horseradish. Spread on toasted bread. Garnish with sprigs of parsley, if desired. Makes ½ cup spread.

Date Roll-Ginger Snips

1 3-ounce package cream cheese,
   softened
1 tablespoon milk
1 tablespoon very finely chopped
   candied ginger
1 8-ounce can date-nut roll

Blend together cream cheese and milk; stir in chopped ginger. Cut date roll into 10 slices. Spread *half* the slices with cream cheese mixture. Top with remaining slices. Cut each sandwich into 4 triangles. Makes 20 appetizers.

Dilled Cucumber Canapés

1 3-ounce package cream
   cheese, softened
1 tablespoon milk
½ teaspoon dried dillweed
¼ teaspoon onion juice
   Dash salt
6 slices white sandwich bread
1 cucumber, thinly sliced

Beat together cream cheese, milk, dillweed, onion juice, and salt. Trim crusts from bread (stack 3 slices for easier trimming). Spread about 1 tablespoon cheese mixture on each slice; cut into triangles. Cut cucumber slices in half; place atop triangles. Garnish with snipped parsley, if desired. Makes 24 canapés.

Corned Beef Appetizers

1 7-ounce can corned beef
1 3-ounce package cream cheese,
   softened
¼ cup milk
1 tablespoon prepared horseradish
   Dash bottled hot pepper sauce
2 tablespoons finely chopped celery
1 tablespoon finely chopped onion
   Melba toast rounds

Flake corned beef. Beat together corned beef, cream cheese, milk, horseradish, and hot pepper sauce till well blended. Stir in celery and onion. Spread corned beef mixture on melba toast rounds. Garnish with sliced pitted ripe olives, if desired. Makes about 36 appetizers.

Classic Antipasto Tray

Mound one 7-ounce can tuna, drained, in center of a large serving tray. Combine ¼ cup mayonnaise or salad dressing and 1 teaspoon lemon juice; spread over tuna. Top with 1 tablespoon drained capers. In spoke-fashion around tuna, arrange thinly sliced salami; thinly sliced boiled ham *or* prosciutto; one 2-ounce can rolled anchovies, drained; mild pickled peppers; pimiento-stuffed green olives; and ripe olives.

Crab-Swiss Bites

1 7½-ounce can crab meat, drained, flaked, and cartilage removed
1 cup shredded Swiss cheese (4 ounces)
½ cup mayonnaise or salad dressing
1 tablespoon sliced green onion
1 teaspoon lemon juice
¼ teaspoon curry powder
1 package refrigerated butterflake rolls (12 rolls)
1 5-ounce can water chestnuts, drained and sliced (⅔ cup)

Combine crab meat, Swiss cheese, mayonnaise, green onion, lemon juice, and curry; mix well. Separate rolls; separate each into three layers. Place on *ungreased* baking sheet; spoon on crab meat mixture. Top each with a few water chestnut slices. Bake at 400° till golden, 10 to 12 minutes. Makes 36 appetizers.

Liver Pâté Appetizers

1 package refrigerated crescent rolls (8 rolls)
2 4¾-ounce cans liver spread
5 slices bacon, crisp-cooked, drained, and crumbled
¼ cup thinly sliced green onion

Separate roll dough at perforations. Generously cover with liver spread; cut each triangle into 4 triangles. Sprinkle bacon and onion over liver; pat in lightly. Roll up, if desired. Place on baking sheet. Bake at 375° about 10 minutes. Serve hot. Makes 32 appetizers.

Blue Cheese-Raisin Canapés

Toast 6 slices raisin bread and trim crusts. Blend together one 3-ounce package cream cheese, softened; ¼ cup crumbled blue cheese; and 1 tablespoon milk. Stir in ½ cup finely chopped walnuts. Spread cheese mixture on toast. Cut each slice diagonally into 4 triangles. Broil on baking sheet 4 inches from heat till lightly browned, about 2 minutes. Garnish with snipped parsley. Makes 24.

Pizza Appetizers

1 package refrigerated butterflake rolls (12 rolls)
1 8-ounce can pizza sauce
½ teaspoon dried oregano, crushed
½ teaspoon dried basil, crushed
4 ounces finely chopped pepperoni
1 cup shredded mozzarella cheese

Separate each roll into 2 layers. Place layers on baking sheet and flatten each to a 3-inch round, forming rim with fingers. Combine pizza sauce, oregano, and basil; stir in pepperoni. Spread about 1 tablespoon mixture on each round. Top with cheese. Bake at 475° till cheese melts, about 8 minutes. Makes 24.

Notches

Hot-style appetizers shown on page 66 —

COST-CUTTING RECIPE

2 ounces Cheddar cheese
24 taco-flavored tortilla chips
½ cup refried beans or canned bean dip
1 canned mild chili pepper, diced

Cut Cheddar cheese in 24 pieces, each ¾ x ¾ x ⅛-inch. Arrange chips on baking sheets. Top each chip with 1 teaspoon beans, a piece of cheese, and a piece of chili pepper. Broil 4 inches from heat till cheese melts, 1 to 3 minutes. Serve hot. Makes 24 appetizers.

Everyone likes them hot

Serving hot appetizers at their best, truly hot, doesn't require a maid or a magician. Just employ the use of good planning and electric appliances. Heat only one round of appetizers at a time, if possible, so hot appetizers will be coming from the oven just as the last batch is eaten. Or, use an electric appliance to keep appetizers hot once they are cooked. An electric portable oven, hot tray, griddle, bun warmer, skillet, slow cooking electric saucepot, or fondue pot will do the job.

Keep a package of refrigerated biscuits and blue cheese on hand, and be prepared to serve *Blue Cheese Bites* to unexpected guests on short notice.

Blue Cheese Bites

1 package refrigerated
   biscuits (10 biscuits)
¼ cup butter or margarine
3 tablespoons crumbled blue cheese

Quarter biscuits; arrange in two 8x1½-inch round baking dishes. Melt butter and cheese together. Drizzle over biscuits. Bake at 400° till browned, 12 to 15 minutes. Makes 40.

Appetizer Twists

Unroll the dough from 1 package refrigerated crescent rolls (8 rolls). Separate into 4 rectangles; press perforations to seal. Brush with 1 tablespoon melted butter or margarine. Sprinkle *half* of the rectangles with 2 tablespoons shredded Cheddar cheese and 2 tablespoons grated Parmesan cheese; sprinkle with garlic powder. Place remaining two rectangles, *buttered side down,* over the cheese. Cut each stack crosswise into twelve ½-inch-wide strips. Twist each strip 4 times. Place on *ungreased* baking sheet; press ends to sheet. Bake at 375° for 10 to 12 minutes. Makes 24.

Bacon-Crescent Roll-Ups

1 package refrigerated crescent rolls
   (8 rolls)
½ cup dairy sour cream
   Onion powder *or* garlic powder
10 to 12 slices bacon, crisp-cooked,
   drained, and crumbled

Unroll crescent rolls and separate triangles. Spread with sour cream; sprinkle *lightly* with onion powder or garlic powder. Top with crumbled bacon. Cut each triangle into 3 equal wedges. Roll up, starting at the point of the wedge. Place roll-ups on greased baking sheet. Bake at 375° till golden brown, 12 to 15 minutes. Serve hot. Makes 24 appetizers.

Tiny Shrimp Rolls

2 5- or 6-ounce packages frozen shrimp
   egg rolls
½ cup grape jelly
½ cup chili sauce
1 teaspoon lemon juice

Cook frozen shrimp egg rolls according to package directions. Cut cocktail-size egg rolls in half and cut large egg rolls into 1-inch slices. In small saucepan combine grape jelly, chili sauce, and lemon juice. Heat, stirring constantly, till grape jelly is melted. Serve jelly mixture as a hot dip for shrimp egg rolls. Makes about 48 appetizers.

Fancy Franks

½ cup chili sauce
½ cup currant jelly
4 teaspoons lemon juice
1½ teaspoons prepared mustard
2 7¼-ounce jars cocktail
   frankfurters, drained
1 13¼-ounce can pineapple chunks,
   drained

In skillet combine chili sauce, jelly, lemon juice, and mustard. Add frankfurters and pineapple. Simmer 15 minutes; stir occasionally. Serve warm with cocktail picks. Serves 4 to 6.

Sweet-Sour Sausages

During warm weather, cook the sausages on a grill and baste with the sauce—

¾ cup sugar
½ cup vinegar
½ cup water
1 tablespoon chopped green pepper
1 tablespoon chopped canned pimiento
¼ teaspoon salt
1 tablespoon cold water
2 teaspoons cornstarch
1 teaspoon paprika
1 8-ounce package brown-and-serve
    sausage links (12 links), halved

In a saucepan combine sugar, vinegar, the ½ cup water, green pepper, pimiento, and salt; simmer 5 minutes. Blend the 1 tablespoon cold water slowly into cornstarch; add to hot mixture. Cook, stirring constantly, till mixture is thickened and bubbly; stir in paprika.

Meanwhile, cook brown-and-serve sausages according to package directions; add to the sugar-vinegar mixture. Heat through. Serve hot with cocktail picks. Makes 24 appetizers.

Parmesan-Potato Bites

Teen-agers will enjoy preparing this appetizer as well as eating it—

½ cup grated Parmesan cheese
    Dash garlic powder
1 16-ounce package frozen fried
    potato nuggets
½ cup butter or margarine, melted
1 8-ounce can pizza sauce
3 tablespoons finely chopped onion
2 tablespoons snipped parsley

Combine the grated Parmesan cheese and garlic powder. Dip the potato nuggets in melted butter or margarine. Roll nuggets in the cheese mixture. Place in a single layer on a greased 15½x10½x1-inch baking pan. Bake at 425° till golden brown, about 12 minutes.

Meanwhile, in a small saucepan cook the pizza sauce, onion, and parsley till heated through. To serve, spear potato nuggets, lengthwise, with wooden picks and use as dippers with hot pizza sauce mixture. Makes about 48.

Garlic-Buttered Shrimp

This seafood appetizer is pictured on page 76—

1 pound fresh or frozen shelled
    jumbo shrimp
¼ cup butter or margarine
1 tablespoon snipped parsley
⅛ teaspoon garlic powder
⅛ teaspoon cayenne
3 tablespoons dry white wine

Thaw frozen shrimp. In saucepan melt butter or margarine. Stir in snipped parsley, garlic powder, and cayenne; cook 1 to 2 minutes. Stir in white wine; heat through. Thread shrimp on small skewers. Broil shrimp 3 to 4 inches from heat till done, about 4 minutes, turning frequently and brushing with butter mixture. Serve hot. Makes 15 to 18 appetizers.

Corned Beef and Cheese Meatballs

1 12-ounce can corned beef
1 cup shredded sharp American cheese
    (4 ounces)
½ cup soft bread crumbs
1 beaten egg
2 tablespoons finely chopped onion
1 tablespoon horseradish mustard

Flake corned beef; combine with cheese, bread crumbs, egg, onion, and horseradish mustard. Mix thoroughly. Shape into 36 balls, using a rounded teaspoon corned beef mixture for each. Place on well-greased baking sheet. Bake at 375° about 12 minutes. Remove to serving plate. Serve hot. Makes 36.

Cheesed Artichoke Bottoms

Drain and rinse two 16-ounce cans artichoke bottoms. Pat dry. Blend one 8-ounce package cream cheese, softened; 2 tablespoons finely chopped green onion; and dash pepper. Spoon about 2 teaspoons cheese mixture into each artichoke, spreading smooth. Sprinkle each with about 1 teaspoon grated Parmesan cheese. Bake on baking sheet at 325° till heated through, 15 to 18 minutes. Garnish with finely chopped green onion tops. Makes about 20.

Appetizers that Wait

Harlequin Sandwiches

Use several different cookie cutters and garnishes for a varied array of appetizers —

> Tuna Filling
> Deviled Ham Filling
> Peanut Butter-Apple Filling
> 8 slices firm-textured white bread
> 8 slices firm-textured rye bread
> 1 4-ounce container whipped cream cheese
> Green pepper strips
> Snipped parsley
> Sliced canned pimiento

Advance preparation: Prepare Tuna Filling, Deviled Ham Filling, and/or Peanut Butter-Apple Filling. Using a cookie or biscuit cutter, cut white and rye bread into shapes. Wrap bread in clear plastic wrap or bags.
Before serving: Spread white bread shapes with Tuna, Deviled Ham, and/or Peanut Butter-Apple Fillings. Top with matching rye bread shapes. Frost tops with whipped cream cheese. Decorate tops of sandwiches with green pepper strips, snipped parsley, and pimiento.

Tuna Filling

Advance preparation: Combine one 6½- or 7-ounce can tuna, drained and flaked; 1 hard-cooked egg, chopped; ¼ cup finely chopped cucumber; ¼ cup finely chopped celery; and 2 tablespoons sweet pickle relish. Blend in ¼ cup mayonnaise or salad dressing and 1 teaspoon lemon juice. Cover and chill mixture till ready to serve. Makes 2¼ cups filling.

Deviled Ham Filling

Advance preparation: Combine one 4½-ounce can deviled ham, ¼ cup finely chopped celery, ¼ cup finely chopped dill pickle, and 1 tablespoon mayonnaise or salad dressing. Cover and chill till ready to serve. Makes 1 cup.

Peanut Butter-Apple Filling

Advance preparation: Blend together ½ cup creamy peanut butter, 2 tablespoons mayonnaise or salad dressing, and 2 teaspoons lemon juice. Stir in ½ cup finely chopped, peeled tart apple and 4 slices bacon, crisp-cooked, drained, and crumbled. Cover and refrigerate.
Before serving: Remove from refrigerator; return to room temperature. Makes 1¼ cups.

Consommé and Cheese Pâté

> 1 teaspoon unflavored gelatin
> 2 tablespoons cold water
> ¾ cup canned condensed beef consommé
> 1 4¾-ounce can liver spread
> 3 tablespoons mayonnaise or salad dressing
> 1 8-ounce package cream cheese, softened
> 3 tablespoons milk
> 1 tablespoon onion soup mix
> Assorted crackers

Advance preparation: In small bowl soften gelatin in cold water. Set in pan of hot water; dissolve gelatin. Stir in consommé. Chill till partially set. Line an 8½x4½x2½-inch loaf pan with waxed paper. Turn consommé mixture into pan; chill till almost set. Combine liver spread and mayonnaise; spread over consommé mixture. Blend cream cheese, milk, and onion soup mix together; spread over liver mixture. Cover and chill overnight.
Before serving: Unmold; remove paper. Pipe additional cream cheese around edges, if desired. Serve with crackers. Makes 2 cups.

Be creative with these appetizers

Fill *Harlequin Sandwiches* with *Tuna Filling, Deviled Ham Filling,* and/or *Peanut Butter-Apple Filling,* then use your imagination to decorate the tops. →

Cheese Log

2 cups shredded sharp Cheddar cheese
   (8 ounces)
1 3-ounce package cream cheese with
   chives
¼ cup dry white wine
1 teaspoon prepared horseradish
   • • •
½ cup chopped smoked beef
   Assorted crackers

Advance preparation: Let Cheddar cheese and cream cheese with chives soften at room temperature. Beat together the cheeses, white wine, and prepared horseradish. Chill 1 hour. Shape mixture into a log about 1½ inches in diameter. Roll log in chopped smoked beef. Wrap and chill until ready to serve. Serve cheese log with crackers. Makes 1¾ cups.

Anchovy-Cheese Ball

Festive appetizer shown on page 66 —

1 8-ounce package cream cheese,
   softened
½ cup butter or margarine, softened
1 tablespoon anchovy paste
1 teaspoon paprika
½ teaspoon caraway seed
½ teaspoon prepared mustard
   Raw vegetables

Advance preparation: In bowl beat cream cheese and butter. Add anchovy paste, paprika, caraway, and mustard; blend well. Line a small bowl with clear plastic wrap; turn mixture into bowl. Cover; chill 4 to 24 hours.
Before serving: Unmold; remove wrap and smooth surface. Garnish with radish slices, if desired. Serve with vegetables. Makes 1½ cups.

Cater to the men in the crowd by serving robust *Pickled Knackwurst* with cold beer. The guys will also like to try their own hand at preparing this knackwurst and onion, pickled cauliflower, and pepper appetizer.

Appetizer Cheesecake

Layered appetizer pictured on page 67 —

   1 cup dairy sour cream
   ¼ cup finely chopped green pepper
   ¼ cup finely chopped celery
   2 tablespoons finely chopped pimiento-
      stuffed green olives
   2 tablespoons finely chopped onion
   1 teaspoon lemon juice
   ½ teaspoon Worcestershire sauce
     Dash paprika
   2 or 3 drops bottled hot pepper sauce
   ⅔ cup finely crushed rich round cheese
      crackers (about 16 crackers)
     Assorted crackers and vegetables

Advance preparation: Thoroughly combine sour cream, green pepper, celery, olives, onion, lemon juice, Worcestershire, paprika, and hot pepper sauce. Line a 2½-cup bowl with clear plastic wrap. Reserve some of the cheese crackers for garnish. Spread about ½ cup sour cream mixture in bowl. Sprinkle with ¼ cup cheese crackers. Repeat sour cream and cracker layers. Cover; chill overnight.
Before serving: Unmold; remove wrap. Top with reserved crackers. Serve spread with crackers and vegetables. Makes about 2 cups.

Clam and Avocado Dip

Tasty appetizer dip shown on page 66 —

   2 ripe avocados, seeded, peeled, and
      cut into pieces
   1 7½-ounce can minced clams, drained
   2 tablespoons mayonnaise or salad
      dressing
   1 tablespoon chopped onion
   1 tablespoon lemon juice
   ½ teaspoon salt
     Dash freshly ground pepper
     Dash garlic salt
     Corn chips or assorted crackers

Advance preparation: In small mixing bowl or blender container combine all ingredients *except* chips. Beat or cover and blend till smooth. Pour into serving bowl. Cover; chill well. Serve with corn chips or crackers as dippers. Makes 1½ cups dip.

Pickled Knackwurst

   1½ pounds fully cooked knackwurst
   1 medium onion, thinly sliced
   2½ cups water
   1¾ cups vinegar
   2 tablespoons sugar
   1 tablespoon pickling spice
   1½ teaspoons salt
   1 teaspoon crushed dried red pepper
   1 teaspoon whole allspice
   ¾ teaspoon whole black pepper
     Pickled cauliflower
     Cherry peppers

Advance preparation: Slice knackwurst diagonally into ½-inch-thick pieces. Separate onion into rings. In 2-quart crock or jar alternate layers of knackwurst and onion. In saucepan heat together water, vinegar, sugar, pickling spice, salt, red pepper, whole allspice, and black pepper till warm. Pour over knackwurst and onion. Cover and chill for 3 days.
Before serving: Thread meat, onion, cauliflower, and cherry peppers on skewers.

Marinated Shrimp Platter

   3 pounds fresh or frozen shrimp in
      shells
   1 cup cooking oil
   1 cup white vinegar
   ¼ cup undrained capers
   1 tablespoon celery seed
   2 teaspoons salt
     Romaine
   1½ cups whole large ripe olives
     Tomato wedges

Advance preparation: Add shrimp to boiling salted water. Reduce heat; simmer till shrimp turn pink, 1 to 3 minutes. Drain and peel. In screw-top jar combine oil, vinegar, capers, celery seed, and salt; cover and shake well. Pour over cooked shrimp in bowl. Cover and chill several hours or overnight.
Before serving: Drain shrimp, reserving marinade. On an oblong platter arrange a bed of romaine. Place shrimp down center. Make a row of olives on both sides. Spoon some reserved marinade over all. Garnish with tomato.

Oriental Shrimp Crepes

    1 beaten egg
    ¾ cup milk
    1 tablespoon butter or margarine,
        melted
    ⅓ cup all-purpose flour
        Dash salt
    ½ of a 4½-ounce can shrimp, drained
        and finely chopped (⅓ cup)
    ⅓ cup dairy sour cream
    ¼ cup shredded carrot
    ¼ cup finely chopped celery
    2 tablespoons dry sherry
    1 tablespoon butter or margarine,
        melted

Advance preparation: Combine egg, milk, and 1 tablespoon butter; add flour and salt. Beat with electric mixer or rotary beater till smooth. Lightly grease a griddle; heat till drop of water sizzles on surface. Pour a scant tablespoon of batter on griddle and shape into a circle, using tip of spoon. (Cook about 3 crepes at a time.) Cook till underside is lightly browned, about 1½ minutes. Turn and cook second side about ½ minute longer. Remove to paper toweling. Repeat to cook remaining crepes.

Combine shrimp, sour cream, carrot, celery, and sherry. Spread about 1½ teaspoons mixture down the middle of each crepe; roll up. Place, seam side down, in greased shallow baking dish. Cover and chill up to 8 hours.
Before serving: Brush lightly with 1 tablespoon melted butter. Bake, uncovered, at 350° for 20 to 25 minutes. Serve warm. Makes 24.

Storing make-ahead appetizers

When making appetizers ahead, follow these suggestions to prevent the food from loosing flavor or quality. After preparing appetizers, chill or freeze the food quickly. Always cover foods completely so they are airtight, and wrap in moisture-vaporproof materials for the freezer. Use food from the refrigerator within 24 hours or the time given in the recipe.

Chicken Appetizer Crepes

    1 beaten egg
    ¾ cup milk
    1 tablespoon butter or
        margarine, melted
    ⅓ cup all-purpose flour
    ½ cup finely chopped cooked chicken *or*
        turkey
    ⅓ cup condensed cream of chicken soup
    ¼ cup cooked chopped spinach
    2 tablespoons coarsely crushed saltine
        crackers (2 crackers)
    2 tablespoons grated Parmesan cheese
    2 tablespoons chopped onion
    1 tablespoon butter or margarine,
        melted

Advance preparation: Combine egg, milk, and 1 tablespoon butter; add flour and dash salt. Beat till smooth. Heat a lightly greased griddle till drop of water sizzles on surface. For each crepe, pour a scant tablespoon batter on griddle and shape into circle with tip of spoon. Cook until underside is lightly browned, about 1½ minutes. Turn and cook second side about ½ minute longer. Remove to paper toweling. Repeat to cook remaining crepes.

Combine chicken, soup, spinach, crackers, cheese, and onion. Spread about 1½ teaspoons mixture down middle of each crepe; roll up. Place, seam side down, in greased shallow baking dish. Cover; chill up to 8 hours.
Before serving: Brush lightly with 1 tablespoon melted butter. Bake, uncovered, at 350° for 20 to 25 minutes. Serve warm. Makes 24 crepes.

Ham-Stuffed Eggs

Advance preparation: Cut 6 hard-cooked eggs in half lengthwise. Remove egg yolks and mash. Blend in 3 tablespoons dairy sour cream, ½ teaspoon prepared mustard, ¼ teaspoon salt, and dash pepper. Stir in ½ cup finely chopped fully cooked ham. Refill whites with yolk mixture. Arrange eggs in buttered 9-inch pie plate. Cover and chill up to 8 hours.
Before serving: Brush eggs with 1 tablespoon melted butter or margarine; sprinkle with paprika. Bake at 375° till hot through, about 15 minutes. Makes 12 appetizers.

Mini Quiches

1 package refrigerated butterflake
    rolls (12 rolls)
1 4½-ounce can shrimp, drained
    (about 1 cup)
1 beaten egg
½ cup light cream
1 tablespoon brandy
½ teaspoon salt
    Dash pepper
1⅓ ounces Gruyère cheese (2 triangles)

Advance preparation: Grease 2 dozen 1¾-inch miniature muffin pans. Divide each roll in half; press into muffin pan to make a pastry shell. Place one shrimp in each shell. Combine egg, cream, brandy, salt, and pepper. Divide mixture evenly among shells, using about 2 teaspoons for each. Cut Gruyère cheese into 24 small triangles; place one atop each appetizer. Bake at 375° till golden, about 20 minutes. Cool; wrap in foil and freeze.
Before serving: Place frozen appetizers on a baking sheet. Bake at 375° for 10 to 12 minutes. Serve warm. Makes 24 appetizers.

Minced Meatballs

2 beaten eggs
⅓ cup fine dry bread crumbs
1 2¼-ounce can deviled ham
½ teaspoon salt
    Dash pepper
1 pound lean ground beef
1 22-ounce can mincemeat pie filling
⅓ cup apple juice *or* apple cider
1 tablespoon vinegar

Advance preparation: Combine eggs, bread crumbs, deviled ham, salt, and pepper; add lean ground beef. Mix well. Shape mixture into 72 tiny meatballs. Place in shallow baking pan. Bake at 375° till done, 12 to 14 minutes. Cool; remove from pan. Cover and chill.
Before serving: Combine pie filling, apple juice or cider, and vinegar. Heat till bubbly. Add meatballs and heat through. Serve in chafing dish with cocktail picks. Keep warm, adding additional apple juice if mixture becomes too thick. Makes 72 appetizers.

Spicy Cocktail Meatballs

1 slightly beaten egg
¼ cup fine dry bread crumbs
1 teaspoon prepared mustard
½ teaspoon salt
⅛ teaspoon pepper
¾ pound ground beef
1 4¾-ounce can liver spread
2 cups corn chips, crushed (¾ cup)

Advance preparation: Combine egg, bread crumbs, mustard, salt, and pepper. Add ground beef and liver spread; mix well. Shape into 1-inch balls, using a rounded teaspoon meat mixture for each. Cover tightly; chill overnight.
Before serving: Roll meatballs in crushed chips. Bake in shallow pan at 350° about 20 minutes. Serve hot. Makes about 60 meatballs.

Hawaiian Ginger-Pork Appetizers

⅔ cup soy sauce
⅔ cup water
½ cup chopped onion
¼ cup sugar
¼ cup dry sherry
1 2-inch piece fresh gingerroot,
    peeled and sliced
1 tablespoon chopped canned green
    chili peppers
1 clove garlic, minced
2 tablespoons cold water
1 tablespoon cornstarch
2 pounds boneless pork, cut into bite-size pieces

Advance preparation: Combine soy sauce, the ⅔ cup water, onion, sugar, sherry, gingerroot, chili peppers, and garlic. Bring to boiling; reduce heat. Cook, uncovered, 20 minutes. Slowly blend the 2 tablespoons cold water into cornstarch; add to soy mixture. Cook and stir till thickened. Strain; discard solids. Cool. Place pork in bowl; pour marinade over. Cover; chill 6 hours, stirring once or twice.
Before serving: Drain pork, reserving marinade. Thread about 3 pieces of pork on each skewer. Broil 3 to 4 inches from heat till pork is done, about 10 minutes, turning and brushing with marinade. Makes about 15 appetizers.

Calorie-Reduced Appetizers

Onion Puffs

18 calories per appetizer—

½ of a 12-ounce carton cream-
style cottage cheese, drained
(¾ cup)
1 teaspoon instant minced onion
¼ teaspoon salt
2 tablespoons grated Parmesan cheese
1 tablespoon finely chopped canned
pimiento
3 drops bottled hot pepper sauce
2 stiffly beaten egg whites
30 melba toast rounds

Combine cream-style cottage cheese, instant minced onion, and salt; beat with rotary beater or electric mixer till smooth. Stir in grated Parmesan cheese, chopped pimiento, and hot pepper sauce. Fold in stiffly beaten egg whites. Spread cheese mixture on melba toast rounds and place on baking sheet. Bake at 450° for 8 to 10 minutes. Makes 30 appetizers.

Shrimp-Cucumber Dip

This appetizer dip, which adds up to only 13 calories per tablespoon, is pictured on page 66—

1 medium cucumber
1 cup cream-style cottage cheese
2 tablespoons finely chopped onion
2 teaspoons vinegar
½ teaspoon prepared horseradish
• • •
1 4½-ounce can shrimp, drained and
coarsely chopped
Vegetable dippers (see tip, page 36)

Cut unpeeled cucumber in half lengthwise; remove seeds and discard. Shred enough cucumber to make 1 cup; drain. In small mixing bowl combine the shredded cucumber, cream-style cottage cheese, chopped onion, vinegar, and horseradish. Beat till smooth with electric mixer. Stir in chopped shrimp. Serve dip with vegetable dippers. Makes about 2 cups.

Cottage-Dill Dip

11 calories per tablespoon—

⅓ cup skim milk
1 to 2 teaspoons dill pickle juice
1 12-ounce carton dry cottage cheese
(1½ cups)
½ teaspoon onion salt
¼ cup finely chopped dill pickle
2 tablespoons finely chopped canned
pimiento
Vegetable dippers (see tip, page 36)

Place milk, pickle juice, cottage cheese, and onion salt in blender container; blend till smooth. Pour into small bowl. Stir in chopped pickle and pimiento. Chill till ready to serve. Serve with vegetables. Makes 2 cups dip.

Curried Chicken Soup

61 calories per serving—

In a small saucepan gradually stir 1¼ cups skim milk into one 10½-ounce can condensed cream of chicken soup. Add ½ cup water, 1 tablespoon snipped parsley, and ½ teaspoon curry powder. Heat till simmering; stir occasionally. Trim with snipped parsley. Serves 6.

French Onion Soup

42 calories per serving—

1 large onion, thinly sliced
1 tablespoon butter or margarine
2 10½-ounce cans condensed beef broth
¾ cup water
½ teaspoon Worcestershire sauce
Dash pepper
1 tablespoon grated Parmesan cheese

Cook onion in butter over medium-low heat till lightly browned, about 20 minutes. Add beef broth, water, and Worcestershire. Bring to boiling; season with pepper. Pour into bowls; sprinkle with cheese. Makes 6 servings.

Mushroom Cocktail

38 calories per serving —

⅓ cup catsup
1 tablespoon vinegar
½ teaspoon prepared horseradish
   Lettuce leaves
1½ cups shredded lettuce
12 fresh medium mushrooms, sliced

In small bowl blend catsup, vinegar, and horseradish. Cover and chill. Line 6 sherbets with lettuce leaves; add shredded lettuce. Arrange mushrooms atop shredded lettuce. Cover; chill. Just before serving, drizzle each with 1 tablespoon catsup mixture. Makes 6 servings.

Spiced Citrus Appetizer Cup

52 calories per serving —

1 16-ounce can mixed grapefruit and orange sections
3 inches stick cinnamon
   Dash ground cloves
   Dash ground ginger

In saucepan combine undrained grapefruit and orange sections, cinnamon, cloves, and ginger. Simmer for 10 minutes. Remove stick cinnamon. Cover and chill. Serve in sherbets. Garnish with mint sprigs, if desired. Serves 5.

Tuna Balls

16 calories per appetizer —

1 7-ounce can water-pack tuna, drained and flaked
1 3-ounce package Neufchâtel cheese, softened
2 tablespoons finely chopped celery
2 teaspoons lemon juice
½ teaspoon Worcestershire sauce
¼ teaspoon salt
⅓ cup finely snipped parsley

Blend tuna and cheese. Add celery, lemon juice, Worcestershire, and salt; mix well. Shape into small balls, using about 2 teaspoons mixture for each. Roll in parsley. Chill well. Serve with cocktail picks. Makes about 30.

Grapefruit-Crab Cocktail

57 calories per serving —

1 7½-ounce can crab meat, chilled, drained, flaked, and cartilage removed
1 tablespoon lemon juice
1 16-ounce can unsweetened grapefruit sections, chilled
⅓ cup catsup
¼ teaspoon dry mustard
¼ teaspoon prepared horseradish
   Dash bottled hot pepper sauce
   Lettuce

Sprinkle crab meat with lemon juice. Drain grapefruit, reserving ¼ cup juice. Combine reserved grapefruit juice, catsup, dry mustard, horseradish, and hot pepper sauce. Cover and chill. Arrange grapefruit sections and crab meat in 8 lettuce-lined sherbets. Drizzle with catsup mixture. Makes 8 servings.

Pickled Shrimp

27 calories per shrimp appetizer —

1 pound fresh or frozen shrimp in shells
¼ cup celery leaves
2 tablespoons mixed pickling spice
1½ teaspoons salt
½ cup sliced onion
4 bay leaves
¾ cup low-calorie Italian salad dressing
⅓ cup white vinegar
1 tablespoon undrained capers
1 teaspoon celery seed
½ teaspoon salt
   Few drops bottled hot pepper sauce

In saucepan cover shrimp with boiling water; add celery leaves, pickling spice, and 1½ teaspoons salt. Cover and simmer for 5 minutes. Drain; peel shrimp under cold water. Combine shrimp, onion, and bay leaves; arrange in shallow dish. Combine remaining ingredients; mix well. Pour over shrimp mixture. Cover; marinate in refrigerator at least 24 hours, spooning marinade over occasionally. Makes about 2½ cups.

First-Course Appetizers

Layered Fruit Compote

¼ cup honey
1 tablespoon lemon juice
1½ teaspoons finely snipped candied
ginger (optional)
½ teaspoon grated orange peel
2 oranges, peeled and sliced
1 cup cubed honeydew melon
¾ cup blueberries
¾ cup halved strawberries
Whole strawberries (optional)

Combine honey, lemon juice, snipped candied ginger, and grated orange peel. Pour honey mixture over orange slices in bowl. Cover and chill several hours. Chill honeydew melon, blueberries, and halved strawberries.

Drain oranges, reserving liquid. Arrange oranges in a compote. Top with a layer of blueberries, then melon and halved strawberries. Pour reserved liquid over all. Garnish with whole strawberries, if desired. Serves 5.

Frosty Fruit Cup

1 13¼-ounce can pineapple chunks
2 7-ounce bottles ginger ale
½ of a 6-ounce can frozen grapefruit
juice concentrate, thawed
(⅓ cup)
1 pint strawberries, halved
1½ cups cantaloupe balls
1 cup seedless green grapes, halved
Mint sprigs (optional)

Drain pineapple chunks, reserving syrup. Combine ginger ale, grapefruit juice concentrate, and reserved pineapple syrup. Pour grapefruit juice mixture into a 4-cup refrigerator tray; freeze till slushy, 3 to 3½ hours. Combine strawberries, cantaloupe, grapes, and pineapple chunks. Cover and chill. Spoon chilled fruit mixture into 8 sherbet glasses. Top with the frozen grapefruit juice mixture. Garnish with mint, if desired. Makes 8 servings.

Champagne Strawberries

An elegant beginning for dinner—

1 pint strawberries, sliced
2 tablespoons sugar
½ cup dry white wine
1 ⅖-pint bottle champagne, chilled

In a bowl combine strawberries and sugar; stir in wine. Cover and chill several hours. Spoon berries and liquid into four 6-ounce goblets. Pour champagne into each. Makes 4 servings.

Rainbow Appetizer

1 cup cubed cantaloupe
1 cup cubed honeydew melon
1 cup watermelon balls
½ cup dry red wine
¼ cup sugar
¼ cup lemon juice
Dash salt

In a bowl combine cantaloupe, honeydew melon, and watermelon. Combine the red wine, sugar, lemon juice, and salt; stir till sugar dissolves. Pour mixture over fruits. Cover and chill 4 hours, stirring occasionally. Spoon fruit mixture and some of the liquid into each of 6 sherbet glasses. Makes 6 servings.

Clam-Tomato Juice Ice

1 16-ounce can clam-tomato
juice cocktail
1 tablespoon lemon juice
5 drops bottled hot pepper sauce
4 lemon slices

Combine clam-tomato juice cocktail, lemon juice, and hot pepper sauce. Pour into 3-cup refrigerator tray; freeze firm. Remove from freezer 15 minutes before serving. Break into slush and spoon into 4 sherbet glasses. Garnish with lemon slices. Makes 4 servings.

Pineapple Shrub

1 12-ounce can pineapple
     juice, chilled (1½ cups)
1 cup apple juice, chilled
1 tablespoon lemon juice
     Pineapple, lemon, *or* orange sherbet
     Mint sprigs (optional)

Combine pineapple juice, apple juice, and lemon juice. Pour into juice glasses. Top each glass with a small scoop of sherbet. If desired, garnish with mint sprigs. Serves 8 to 10.

Broiled Orange Halves

3 large oranges
1 tablespoon butter or margarine
2 tablespoons grenadine
     Ground cinnamon

Cut oranges in half crosswise. If necessary, cut off thin slice from bottom of each half so oranges sit evenly on baking sheet. Cut completely around and under orange pulp to loosen from shells. Cut across pulp into 6 to 8 wedges. Dot each orange half with ½ teaspoon butter or margarine; drizzle each with 1 teaspoon grenadine. Sprinkle with cinnamon. Broil 4 inches from heat till tops are bubbly, 4 to 5 minutes. Serve hot. Makes 6 servings.

Artichokes Continental

4 small artichokes
1 2-ounce jar red caviar
1 cup dairy sour cream

Cut 1 inch from top of artichokes; pull off loose leaves around bottom. Slice off stem close to base. Snip off sharp leaf tips with scissors. Cook in boiling salted water till stem is tender and a leaf pulls easily from base, 25 to 30 minutes. Place, upside down, on rack to drain thoroughly and cool slightly. Pull out the middle leaves; remove the choke (fuzzy portion). Chill. Reserve 1 tablespoon caviar. Stir remaining caviar into sour cream; spoon sour cream mixture into artichokes. Top with reserved caviar. Makes 4 servings.

Serve *Artichokes Continental* as the first course for special occasions. This elegant artichoke-sour cream-caviar appetizer is easy to prepare.

Avocado with Marinated Shrimp

1 pound frozen shelled shrimp
½ cup white wine vinegar
½ cup dry white wine
⅓ cup olive oil
⅓ cup chopped onion
1 tablespoon pickling spice
1 tablespoon dried parsley flakes
1 tablespoon sugar
4 avocados
     Lemon juice

Cook shrimp according to package directions; drain. In saucepan combine vinegar, wine, olive oil, onion, pickling spice, parsley, sugar, and 1 teaspoon salt. Bring to a boil; reduce heat and simmer 3 minutes. Pour over shrimp. Cover; chill several hours. Stir occasionally. Halve unpeeled avocados; remove seeds. Brush with lemon juice; sprinkle with salt. Drain shrimp; brush lightly to remove spices and herbs. Spoon into avocado shells. Serves 8.

Bacon-Stuffed Avocados

    4 avocados
      Lemon juice
    8 slices bacon, crisp-cooked, drained,
      and crumbled
    ½ cup butter or margarine
    ¼ cup sugar
    ¼ cup catsup
    ¼ cup wine vinegar
    1 tablespoon soy sauce

Cut unpeeled avocados in half; remove seeds. Brush with lemon juice. Fill with crumbled bacon. Combine butter or margarine, sugar, catsup, wine vinegar, and soy sauce; heat to boiling. Spoon warm butter mixture over filled avocado halves. Makes 8 servings.

Artichoke-Crab Bisque

    2 artichokes
    1 13¾-ounce can chicken broth
    ½ cup whipping cream
    1 egg yolk
    2 tablespoons all-purpose flour
    ¼ teaspoon salt
    ½ cup finely chopped carrot
    2 tablespoons sliced green onion
    ¼ cup water
    1 7½-ounce can crab meat, drained,
      flaked, and cartilage removed
    2 teaspoons lemon juice

Remove and discard two or three layers of outer artichoke leaves. Cut stems to ½ inch. Quarter artichokes. Cook, covered, in boiling salted water till tender, 15 to 20 minutes. Drain; remove leaves. Remove pulp from each leaf by scraping firmly across base with blade of knife. Repeat to be sure all pulp is removed; discard leaves. Remove and discard choke (fuzzy portion). Place chicken broth, cream, egg yolk, flour, and salt in blender container. Add artichoke bottom and pulp from leaves. Cover; blend just enough to puree. In large saucepan cook carrot and green onion, covered, in the ¼ cup water till tender, about 5 minutes. Add artichoke purée. Cook and stir till thickened and bubbly. Stir in crab meat and lemon juice; heat through. Serves 8.

Tomato-Avocado Bisque

    3 tablespoons finely chopped celery
    3 tablespoons finely chopped onion
    2 tablespoons butter or margarine
    1 11-ounce can condensed bisque
      of tomato soup
    1 10½-ounce can condensed
      chicken broth
 1¾ cups water
    1 small avocado, peeled and diced
    2 tablespoons lemon juice

In saucepan cook celery and onion in butter till tender but not brown. Add bisque of tomato soup and chicken broth; stir in water. Simmer 10 minutes. Stir in diced avocado and lemon juice; heat through. Makes 8 servings.

Egg Shred-Corn Soup

    1 12-ounce can whole kernel corn
    1 10½-ounce can condensed
      chicken broth
    ½ cup water
    2 eggs
    2 tablespoons snipped parsley

In medium saucepan combine whole kernel corn, condensed chicken broth, and water; bring to boiling. Beat eggs just till combined. Stir broth mixture so that it is swirling in the saucepan. Very gradually pour eggs through a narrow funnel into the soup, *stirring the mixture quickly* with a fork. Continue till all the egg is added and cooked in fine shreds. Ladle hot soup into soup bowls; top each serving with snipped parsley. Makes 4 servings.

Sherried Beef Broth

    4 cups beef broth
    1 cup thinly sliced fresh mushrooms
    ½ cup dry sherry
    ½ teaspoon salt

In saucepan combine the beef broth and mushrooms. Bring to boiling; simmer for 2 minutes. Add the sherry and salt; heat through, but *do not boil.* Makes 6 to 8 servings.

Lemon and Egg Soup

4 cups chicken broth
¼ cup long grain rice
1 well-beaten egg
1 to 2 tablespoons lemon juice

In saucepan bring broth and uncooked rice to boiling; reduce heat. Cover and cook till rice is tender, 15 to 20 minutes. Stir a moderate amount of hot mixture into beaten egg; return to saucepan. Cook and stir over low heat till slightly thickened, 1 to 2 minutes longer. Add lemon juice to taste. Makes 8 servings.

Stracciatella

2 13¾-ounce cans chicken broth
    (3½ cups)
¼ cup tripolini (tiny bow tie-shaped pasta)
1 slightly beaten egg
2 tablespoons grated Parmesan cheese
2 teaspoons snipped parsley
    Dash ground nutmeg

In saucepan bring broth and tripolini to a boil. Reduce heat; simmer, covered, till pasta is tender, 10 to 15 minutes. Mix remaining ingredients; gradually pour into simmering broth, whipping gently with wire whisk or fork till blended. Serve immediately. Serves 6.

Fruit Cocktail Soup

1 17-ounce can fruit cocktail
2 tablespoons cornstarch
1 cup orange juice
½ cup raisins *or* dried currants
    Dash ground nutmeg
2 tablespoons orange liqueur

Drain fruit cocktail, reserving syrup. Add water to reserved syrup to make 1 cup. In medium saucepan blend syrup slowly into cornstarch. Add fruit cocktail, orange juice, raisins, and nutmeg. Cook and stir till mixture thickens and bubbles; stir in liqueur. Serve warm or cold. Garnish with dollops of dairy sour cream, if desired. Makes 4 or 5 servings.

Creamy Watercress Soup

1 13¾-ounce can chicken broth
1 tablespoon cornstarch
20 watercress stems, each about 3 inches long
½ cup watercress leaves
1 cup light cream
2 tablespoons butter or margarine
1 teaspoon lemon juice

Blend ¼ *cup* of the chicken broth slowly into cornstarch; set aside. In saucepan combine remaining broth and watercress stems; bring to boiling. Reduce heat; simmer 5 minutes. Stir in cornstarch mixture. Cook and stir over medium heat till boiling. Pour broth mixture into blender container; add watercress leaves. Cover and blend on low speed till watercress stems and leaves are chopped. Return to saucepan; stir in cream, butter, and lemon juice. Heat to boiling. Season to taste with salt and pepper. Serve at once or chill. Serves 5 or 6.

Chilled Avocado-Bacon Soup

In blender container combine one 10½-ounce can condensed chicken broth; one 7¾-ounce can frozen avocado dip, thawed; ¼ cup water; and 1 tablespoon lemon juice. Cover; blend till smooth. Add 1 cup dairy sour cream, a little at a time, blending at low speed till smooth. Cover and chill well. Crisp-cook, drain, and crumble 6 slices bacon. Pour broth mixture into chilled icers or small soup bowls. Sprinkle with bacon and snipped parsley. Serves 4 to 6.

Chilled Cucumber-Tomato Soup

1 10¾-ounce can condensed tomato soup
1 soup can milk (1¼ cups)
1 medium cucumber, peeled and shredded
2 tablespoons sliced green onion
½ teaspoon Worcestershire sauce

Combine soup, milk, cucumber, onion, Worcestershire, 1 teaspoon salt, and dash pepper. Cover; chill several hours. Serves 4.

Oyster Appetizer

The oysters are cooked briefly, then topped with a tangy chili sauce and mayonnaise mixture—

2 cups water
1 teaspoon salt
1 pint shucked oysters, drained
• • •
½ cup mayonnaise or salad dressing
2 tablespoons chili sauce
2 tablespoons chopped green pepper
1 tablespoon sliced green onion with tops
1 teaspoon Worcestershire sauce
⅛ teaspoon salt
Lettuce (optional)

In saucepan bring water and the 1 teaspoon salt to a simmer. Add oysters; simmer (do not boil) till oysters begin to curl around the edges and become plump and firm, 1 to 4 minutes depending on size of oysters. Drain oysters and chill. Combine mayonnaise, chili sauce, green pepper, green onion, Worcestershire, and the ⅛ teaspoon salt. Chill thoroughly. Place oysters in lettuce-lined cocktail glasses and spoon sauce over tops, *or* serve oysters with cocktail picks and dip in sauce. Serves 6.

For an unforgettable appetizer, serve *Peppy Clam Shells* balanced on a bed of oven-heated rock salt. Another time, serve larger portions as a main dish.

Oyster Cocktail

1 pint shucked oysters
1 small onion, thinly sliced
½ cup wine vinegar
2 tablespoons mixed pickling spice
1 tablespoon sugar
1 tablespoon cooking oil
Lettuce

Simmer the oysters in their liquor till the edges curl, 1 to 4 minutes. Drain oysters, reserving ½ cup liquor. Combine reserved liquor, onion, vinegar, pickling spice, sugar, and oil. Bring to boiling; simmer 5 minutes. Pour over oysters. Cover; chill overnight.

To serve, drain oysters and onion. Line 6 cocktail glasses with lettuce. Divide oysters and onion among glasses. Makes 6 servings.

Peppy Clam Shells

½ cup finely chopped onion
½ cup finely chopped celery
¼ cup finely chopped green pepper
¼ cup butter or margarine
2 tablespoons all-purpose flour
1 tablespoon grated Parmesan cheese
¼ teaspoon salt
Dash pepper
Dash Worcestershire sauce
Dash bottled hot pepper sauce
½ cup finely crushed rich round crackers (12 crackers)
1 7½-ounce can minced clams
1 tablespoon butter or margarine, melted

In medium skillet cook onion, celery, and green pepper in the ¼ cup butter till tender but not brown. Stir in flour, cheese, salt, pepper, Worcestershire sauce, and hot pepper sauce. Add ¼ *cup* of the crackers; mix well. Stir in the undrained clams; cook and stir till thickened and bubbly. Divide among 6 baking shells or individual baking dishes. Combine remaining crackers and melted butter; sprinkle atop mixture in each shell. Bake at 350° till heated through, about 15 minutes. Garnish with cherry tomatoes and parsley, if desired. Makes 6 servings.

Avocado-Shrimp Cocktail

 1 3-ounce package cream cheese,
   softened
 2 tablespoons chili sauce
 1 tablespoon lemon juice
 1 teaspoon grated onion
 1 teaspoon Worcestershire sauce
 ½ pound fresh or frozen shelled
   shrimp, cooked and chilled
 1 large avocado, peeled and cubed
 ½ cup sliced celery
   Lettuce

Blend first 5 ingredients and ¼ teaspoon salt till smooth. Chill well. Combine shrimp, avocado, and celery; spoon into 4 lettuce-lined sherbets. Top with sauce. Serves 4.

Yucatan Shrimp Appetizer

 1 cup coarsely chopped seeded tomato
 ½ cup finely chopped onion
 ¼ cup chopped cilanto* or snipped
   parsley
 1 to 2 tablespoons finely chopped
   canned hot green chili peppers,
   seeded
 2 tablespoons cooking oil
 2 tablespoons lime juice
 1 cup shredded lettuce
 1 pound fresh or frozen shelled large
   shrimp, cooked and chilled

Combine first 6 ingredients, ½ teaspoon salt, and dash pepper. Cover; chill. Place lettuce in 8 cocktail glasses; arrange shrimp atop. Spoon tomato mixture over shrimp. Serves 8.
*Also known as coriander or Chinese parsley.

Shrimp in Beer

In saucepan combine 2 pounds fresh or frozen shrimp in shells and three 12-ounce cans beer. Bring to a boil; add 2 dried red peppers, 1 bay leaf, and dash dried thyme, crushed. Simmer, covered, till shrimp is bright pink, about 5 minutes. Drain; cool slightly. Shell shrimp; chill well. Arrange shrimp in individual icers or cocktail glasses. Makes 6 to 8 servings.

Snails with Lemon Butter

 ½ cup butter or margarine, softened
 3 tablespoons lemon juice
 1 tablespoon thinly sliced green onion
 1 tablespoon snipped parsley
 ⅛ teaspoon salt
   Dash pepper
 1 4½-ounce can snails (24 snails)
 24 snail shells
   French bread or individual
   French rolls

Combine butter, lemon juice, green onion, parsley, salt, and pepper; blend together. Thoroughly drain snails. Spoon about ½ teaspoon butter mixture into each snail shell. Add a snail and about ½ teaspoon more butter mixture. Place 6 filled shells on each of 4 snail dishes. (Or, place filled snail shells, open end up, in 8x8x2-inch baking dish.) Bake at 400° till bubbly, about 10 minutes.

To eat, secure shell with snail holder and remove snail from shell with special snail fork or small cocktail fork. Dip French bread into lemon butter from the snail shell. Serves 4.

Turkey-Olive Cocktail

This first-course cocktail is shown on the cover—

 ⅓ cup plain yogurt
 ⅓ cup dairy sour cream
 1 teaspoon lemon juice
 ½ teaspoon salt
   Dash pepper
 1½ cups cubed cooked turkey or chicken
 1 small tomato, seeded and chopped
 ¼ cup sliced pitted ripe olives
 3 tablespoons sliced green onion
   with tops
   Shredded lettuce
   Endive (optional)

In mixing bowl blend together the plain yogurt, sour cream, lemon juice, salt, and pepper. Stir in cubed turkey or chicken, chopped tomato, sliced ripe olives, and green onion. Cover and chill thoroughly. Place shredded lettuce in 8 individual icers or cocktail glasses. Spoon turkey mixture atop lettuce. Garnish with endive, if desired. Makes 8 servings.

Beverages that Go with Appetizers

Eggnog

12 eggs
½ cup sugar
1 quart cold milk
½ to ¾ cup light rum
½ cup bourbon
¼ teaspoon salt
2 cups whipping cream
Ground nutmeg

Separate eggs. In small mixing bowl beat egg yolks. Gradually add sugar and beat till thick and lemon-colored. Add milk, rum, bourbon, and salt. Whip cream. In very large bowl beat egg whites till stiff peaks form. Fold yolk mixture and whipped cream into egg whites. Serve at once in chilled punch bowl. Sprinkle with nutmeg. Makes 25 five-ounce servings.

Brandied Coffee Nog

2 slightly beaten egg yolks
1½ cups milk
1 cup light cream
2 tablespoons light corn syrup
4 teaspoons instant coffee crystals
⅓ cup brandy
¼ cup light corn syrup
¼ cup water
2 egg whites

In large saucepan combine egg yolks, milk, light cream, the 2 tablespoons light corn syrup, and instant coffee crystals. Heat and stir till mixture thickens slightly and almost boils. Remove from heat; stir in brandy. In small saucepan heat the ¼ cup light corn syrup and the water to boiling. Simmer, uncovered, 1 to 2 minutes. Beat egg whites to soft peaks. Gradually add the hot syrup-water mixture, beating till stiff peaks form. Fold egg white mixture into coffee mixture. Pour into mugs. Makes about 8 six-ounce servings.

Apple Cider Wine

3 cups apple cider *or* apple juice
¼ cup sugar
3 inches stick cinnamon
6 whole cloves
Peel of ¼ lemon, cut in strips
1 ⅘-quart bottle dry white wine
2 tablespoons lemon juice

In saucepan combine apple cider, sugar, cinnamon, cloves, and lemon peel. Bring to boiling, stirring till sugar is dissolved. Simmer, uncovered, for 15 minutes; strain to remove spices and peel, if desired. Add wine and lemon juice. Heat through, but do not boil. Serve in warm mugs. Makes 6 eight-ounce servings.

Rosy Champagne Punch

2 16-ounce cans pitted dark sweet cherries
1 12-ounce can pineapple juice (1½ cups)
½ cup brandy
¼ cup lemon juice
• • •
2 ⅘-quart bottles champagne, chilled

Drain cherries, reserving 2 tablespoons liquid. Combine cherries, pineapple juice, brandy, lemon juice, and the reserved cherry liquid. Chill thoroughly to blend flavors. Just before serving, pour into punch bowl; carefully add champagne, pouring down side of bowl. Makes 16 five-ounce servings.

Special-occasion beverages

At your next party offer guests their choice of flavorful *Apple Cider Wine* served in mugs or bubbling *Rosy Champagne Punch* from the punch bowl. →

Coffee Punch

¼ cup sugar
2 tablespoons instant coffee crystals
1 teaspoon vanilla
6 cups milk
¼ cup crème de cacao *or* orange liqueur
½ cup whipping cream
1 quart vanilla ice cream
    Ground nutmeg

Combine sugar, coffee, vanilla, and dash salt; add milk and crème de cacao or orange liqueur. Stir till sugar dissolves. Chill. Whip the cream. Ladle ice cream into punch bowl; pour coffee mixture over. Top with whipped cream and sprinkle with nutmeg. Makes 12 servings.

Bubbling Holiday Punch

1 10-ounce package frozen
    strawberries, thawed
2 limes, thinly sliced
2 cups light rum
2 6-ounce cans frozen daiquiri mix
3 ⅘-quart bottles cold duck

For ice ring, pour water into a ring mold to depth of one inch; freeze. Arrange strawberries and lime slices around mold; add enough water to anchor fruit to ice. Freeze. Fill mold with water; freeze solid.

To serve, in punch bowl combine rum and daiquiri mix. Carefully add ice ring. Pour in cold duck. Makes 20 five-ounce servings.

Mulled Orange Punch

1 46-ounce can orange Hawaiian fruit
    punch
1 46-ounce can apricot nectar
½ lemon, sliced
8 inches stick cinnamon
6 whole allspice

In large saucepan combine all ingredients. Bring to boiling. Cover and simmer 10 minutes. Remove from heat; let stand 30 minutes. Reheat; strain to remove whole spices and lemon slices. Makes 20 five-ounce servings.

Champagne Party Punch

Place assorted fresh fruits such as cranberries, orange wedges, and grapes on foil-lined baking sheet. Freeze fruits till solid. In punch bowl combine two ⅘-quart bottles sauterne, chilled, and 3 cups cognac, chilled. Resting bottles on rim of bowl, carefully pour in six ⅘-quart bottles champagne, chilled, and two 28-ounce bottles carbonated water, chilled. Add frozen fruits. Makes 60 five-ounce servings.

Brandy-Milk Punch

2 cups milk
¾ cup brandy
3 tablespoons anisette
1 egg white
½ teaspoon vanilla
¼ cup powdered sugar
½ teaspoon freshly grated nutmeg
4 ice cubes
    Freshly grated nutmeg (optional)

In blender container combine milk, brandy, anisette, egg white, vanilla, powdered sugar, the ½ teaspoon grated nutmeg, and ice cubes. Cover and blend till frothy. To serve, pour into tall glasses; garnish with freshly grated nutmeg, if desired. Makes 4 or 5 servings.

Spicy Cranberry Punch

¼ cup red cinnamon candies
4 cups water
8 cups cranberry juice cocktail,
    chilled (2 quarts)
1 6-ounce can frozen limeade
    concentrate (⅔ cup)
1 6-ounce can frozen orange juice
    concentrate (⅔ cup)
    Ice chunk

In small saucepan melt candies in water over low heat; chill well. At serving time, combine candy mixture, cranberry juice cocktail, limeade concentrate, and orange juice concentrate in punch bowl. Stir to dissolve frozen concentrates. Float ice chunk in punch bowl. Makes about 18 five-ounce servings.

Sunny Day Punch

> 2 12-ounce cans pineapple juice
> 1 6-ounce can frozen orange juice
>   concentrate, thawed (⅔ cup)
> 1 6-ounce can frozen lemonade
>   concentrate, thawed (⅔ cup)
> 2 ⅘-quart bottles champagne,
>   chilled

Combine pineapple juice, orange juice concentrate, lemonade concentrate, and 4 cups water. Chill thoroughly. Just before serving, transfer to punch bowl; carefully pour champagne down side of bowl. Stir gently. Garnish with orange slices and mint leaves, if desired. Makes 32 five-ounce servings.

Slow Torpedo Punch

> 1 ⅘-quart bottle vodka
> 3 6-ounce cans pink lemonade
>   concentrate, thawed
> 6 12-ounce cans mild beer, chilled
>   Fruited Ice Ring

In punch bowl combine vodka, pink lemonade concentrate, and 7 cups cold water. Just before serving, add beer and Fruited Ice Ring. Makes about 35 five-ounce servings.

Fruited Ice Ring: Alternate canned peach slices and maraschino cherries in bottom of ring mold. Fill with cold water. Freeze.

Frosty Spiced Tea

> ¼ cup sugar
> 6 inches stick cinnamon, broken
> ½ teaspoon whole cloves
> ¼ teaspoon ground nutmeg
> 4 cups boiling water
> 6 teaspoons loose tea *or* 6 tea bags
>   Ice cubes

In saucepan combine the sugar, spices, and ¾ cup water. Cover and simmer for 20 minutes. Strain to remove spices. Pour the boiling water over tea and steep for 4 minutes; strain. Add the sugar mixture and pour over ice cubes in glasses. Makes 6 servings.

Lime-Frosted Punch

> 2 cups sugar
> 3 envelopes unsweetened lemon-lime
>   flavored soft drink powder
> 3 cups pineapple-grapefruit drink,
>   chilled
> ⅓ cup lemon juice
> 1 quart lime sherbet
> 1 32-ounce bottle lemon-lime
>   carbonated beverage, chilled

In punch bowl combine sugar and soft drink powder. Add pineapple-grapefruit drink, lemon juice, and 6 cups cold water; stir till sugar dissolves. Stir *half* of the sherbet to soften; blend into pineapple mixture. Scoop remaining sherbet atop. Resting bottle on rim of bowl, carefully pour in carbonated beverage; stir gently. Makes 36 servings.

Beverage dress-ups

Use one of the following extra touches to give beverages a festive look:
- Garnish lime- and lemon-flavored drinks or punches with spears of fresh pineapple.
- Stud orange, lemon, or lime slices with whole cloves and float atop punches.
- For sweet drinks, wet glass rims with orange or lemon slices, then dip rims in plain or colored granulated sugar.
- Garnish gin- or vodka-based drinks with olives stuffed with anchovies, almonds, tiny onions, or blue cheese.
- Adorn martinis with tiny ears of pickled corn, dilled beans, or pickled pearl onions.
- To avoid diluting drinks, freeze soda water, tonic, or carbonated beverages in cube shapes and use instead of ice.
- Freeze cranberries, small lemon wedges, or berries in ice cubes. First, fill the refrigerator tray half full of water and freeze. Then, add fruit and fill to top of tray with water; freeze solid.
- During the summer months, allow enough freezer space to keep tall glasses or mugs chilled for cold drinks.

Pineapple Sparkle Punch

        2 46-ounce cans pineapple juice
        3 cups orange juice
     1½ cups lemon juice
        ⅓ cup lime juice
     2½ cups sugar
        Ice
        4 28-ounce bottles ginger ale, chilled
        2 28-ounce bottles carbonated water,
           chilled
        Orange and lime slices (optional)

Combine the juices and sugar; chill several hours. Just before serving, place ice in a large punch bowl. Resting bottles on rim, carefully pour in ginger ale and carbonated water. Float orange and lime slices atop the punch, if desired. Makes about 75 servings.

Spiced Viennese Coffee

        2 tablespoons instant espresso coffee
           powder
        2 tablespoons sugar
        7 whole cloves
        2 inches stick cinnamon

In medium saucepan combine coffee powder, sugar, cloves, stick cinnamon, and 3 cups hot water; bring to boiling. Remove from heat; let stand 5 minutes. Remove spices with slotted spoon. Reheat coffee mixture; pour into demitasse cups. If desired, garnish with a dollop of whipped cream and sprinkle generously with ground cinnamon. Makes 6 servings.

Spiced Tea

Combine 3 cups loose orange pekoe tea; ¼ cup shredded orange peel; 4 inches stick cinnamon, coarsely crushed; 1 tablespoon finely chopped candied ginger; and 2 teaspoons whole cloves, coarsely crushed. Heat, covered, in 300° oven for 15 to 20 minutes. Spoon into jar with tight-fitting lid. Seal. Store in cool place at least one week. To prepare tea, use 1 to 2 teaspoons mixture for each 6 cups boiling water; let steep 2 to 3 minutes. Makes 3 cups tea mixture.

Lime Fizz

        2 jiggers gin (3 ounces)
        ¼ cup frozen limeade concentrate,
           thawed
        2 teaspoons white crème de menthe
        1 drop green food coloring
        2 teaspoons fine granulated sugar
        2 cups crushed ice
              • • •
        1 7-ounce bottle carbonated water,
           chilled
        Mint leaves

In blender container combine gin, limeade concentrate, white crème de menthe, green food coloring, and sugar; add ice. Cover; blend for a few seconds. Divide mixture evenly into two highball glasses. Fill with carbonated water. Stir gently with up-and-down motion. Trim with mint leaves. Makes 2 servings.

Mint Sparkle

Mint jelly and ginger ale add a special tingle to this beverage (shown on page 103)—

        1 10-ounce jar mint-flavored apple
           jelly (about 1 cup)
     1½ cups water
        2 12-ounce cans pineapple juice
           (3 cups)
        ½ cup lemon juice
        Ice cubes
        1 28-ounce bottle ginger ale, chilled
        Mint sprigs (optional)

Place mint-flavored apple jelly in saucepan; add the water. Heat and stir over low heat till jelly melts. Cool. Add the pineapple juice and lemon juice. Chill. To serve, place ice cubes in 10 glasses; fill half full with pineapple mixture. Carefully fill remaining half with ginger ale. Stir to blend. Garnish with mint, if desired. Makes 10 servings.

Cold Duck

For each serving, combine one part chilled champagne and one part chilled sparkling Burgundy in a champagne glass.

Buttered Cranberry Cocktail

Some wintry evening, offer a warm welcome to friends by serving a mug of this hot punch—

> 2 48-ounce bottles cranberry juice
>   cocktail (12 cups)
> 1 cup packed brown sugar
> 9 whole cardamom pods, shelled
> 4 inches stick cinnamon
> ½ teaspoon ground allspice
> 2 cups brandy
> 1 cup bourbon
>   Butter or margarine
>   Stick cinnamon (optional)

In large kettle or Dutch oven combine the cranberry juice cocktail and brown sugar; stir till the sugar dissolves. Add the cardamom seeds, the 4 inches stick cinnamon, and allspice. Heat to boiling; reduce heat and simmer 15 minutes. Remove from heat; strain through sieve to remove whole spices.

Stir in the brandy and bourbon. Serve in small mugs. Add a pat of butter or margarine. Serve with cinnamon stick stirrer, if desired. Makes about 20 five-ounce servings.

Spiced Percolator Punch

Cranberry and pineapple juices perk through a coffee maker basket filled with spices—

> 2 32-ounce bottles cranberry juice
>   cocktail
> 1 46-ounce can pineapple juice
> 2 cups water
> 1 cup packed brown sugar
> ¼ teaspoon salt
> 4 teaspoons whole cloves
> 12 inches stick cinnamon, broken in
>   pieces
>   Peel of ¼ orange, cut in strips
> 3 cups light rum

In a 24-cup automatic percolator combine the cranberry juice cocktail, pineapple juice, water, brown sugar, and salt. Place the whole cloves, stick cinnamon pieces, and orange peel in coffee maker basket. Assemble the coffee maker; plug in and percolate.

Just before serving, remove basket and add rum. Makes about 25 six-ounce servings.

Buttered Lemon Punch

> 1 46-ounce can lemon-pink Hawaiian
>   fruit punch
> 12 inches stick cinnamon
> 3 whole allspice
> 1 whole nutmeg
>   • • •
> ¼ cup brandy
> 8 teaspoons butter or margarine

In saucepan heat together punch, stick cinnamon, allspice, and nutmeg till hot, about 10 minutes. Strain to remove whole spices. Return punch mixture to saucepan; add brandy and heat. Pour into mugs. Top *each* with *1 teaspoon* of the butter. Makes 8 servings.

Buttered Wine

> 2 cups muscatel
> 2 cups water
> 1 6-ounce can frozen orange juice
>   concentrate
> 2 tablespoons sugar
> 1 tablespoon butter or margarine
> ⅛ teaspoon ground cinnamon
> ⅛ teaspoon ground nutmeg
>   Lemon slices (optional)

In saucepan combine all ingredients *except* lemon slices. Heat mixture to steaming hot, stirring occasionally. Do not boil. Garnish punch with lemon slices, if desired. Serve at once. Makes 8 five-ounce servings.

Spiced Bourbon-Apple Punch

> 3 cups apple juice
> 1 tablespoon raisins
> 6 inches stick cinnamon
> 6 lemon slices
>   • • •
> 1 cup bourbon

In saucepan combine apple juice, raisins, cinnamon, and lemon slices. Bring to boiling. Remove stick cinnamon. Pour bourbon into each of six 8-ounce mugs. Add hot apple mixture and stir gently. Serve immediately. Serves 6.

Irish Coffee

¼ cup sugar
1½ cups Irish whiskey
6 cups strong hot coffee
½ cup whipping cream

For each serving, place *1½ teaspoons* sugar in serving glass or cup. Pour in *1½ ounces* whiskey, then fill glass with coffee, stirring to dissolve sugar. Whip cream; spoon about *1 tablespoon* atop each. Makes 8 servings.

Tomato Beers

2 16-ounce cans beer, chilled
2 cups hot-style tomato juice
6 green onions

Pour two parts beer to one part tomato juice into each of 6 glasses. Place a green onion in each glass for stirrer. Makes 6 servings.

Margarita

⅔ jigger tequila (1 ounce)
Dash Triple Sec
Juice of ½ lime
½ cup crushed or cracked ice

In blender container combine tequila, Triple Sec, and lime juice. Add ice; cover and blend to mix. Strain into salt-rimmed cocktail glass prepared by rubbing glass rim with cut lime and dipping in salt. Makes 1 serving.

Summer Sangaree

¾ cup light corn syrup
⅓ cup lemon juice
8 drops yellow food coloring
2 7-ounce bottles carbonated water
Ice cubes
2 cups port

Blend corn syrup, lemon juice, and food coloring; stir in carbonated water. Divide mixture among 4 tall glasses. Add ice; carefully pour ½ *cup* port down side of *each* glass. Serves 4.

Citrus-Bourbon Slush

2 tea bags
1 cup boiling water
1 cup sugar
1 6-ounce can frozen orange juice concentrate, thawed (⅔ cup)
½ cup bourbon
½ of a 6-ounce can frozen lemonade concentrate, thawed (⅓ cup)

Steep tea in boiling water for 2 to 3 minutes; remove tea bags. Stir in sugar. Add remaining ingredients and 3½ cups water; mix till sugar is dissolved. Pour into refrigerator trays; freeze firm. Remove from freezer about 10 minutes before serving. Spoon into cocktail glasses; garnish with lemon wedges, if desired. Keep unused portion in freezer. Makes 6 cups.

Tomato-Vermouth Cocktail

2 cups tomato juice, chilled
½ cup dry vermouth
1 tablespoon lemon juice
Ice

In shaker or screw-top jar combine tomato juice, vermouth, and lemon juice; adjust lid. Shake well and chill. Serve with ice. Garnish with lemon wedge, if desired. Serves 4.

Rosé Frappé

1 ⅘-quart bottle rosé
1 6-ounce can frozen lemonade concentrate, thawed
Crushed ice

Combine rosé, concentrate, and ¾ cup water. Pour over crushed ice in sherbets. Garnish with maraschino cherry, if desired. Serves 8.

Sparkling cocktail beverages

As guests arrive, greet them with refreshing *Tomato-Vermouth Cocktail, Summer Sangaree,* delicate *Rosé Frappé,* or *Mint Sparkle* (see recipe, page 100).

Party Menus

Turn to the menus in this chart for help in deciding what kind of party to give and what foods to serve. You'll find snack, appetizer, and beverage recipes for all types of occasions, plus planning hints, table setting ideas, and serving suggestions with each menu.

Holiday Open House (Serves 24)

Consommé and Cheese Pâté (page 82)
Assorted crackers
Cheese Boreck (page 73)
Minced Meatballs (page 87)
Orange Fondant-Stuffed Dates (page 29)
Spritz Cookies (page 29)
Champagne Party Punch (page 98)
Coffee

For a festive holiday centerpiece, fill a brandy snifter with colored glass balls and surround the snifter with evergreen boughs. To make last-minute preparation easier, assemble cheese appetizers early in the day, then bake them in several batches as needed.

Poker Party (Serves 4)

Hot Bean and Cheese Dip (page 37)
Corn chips   Tortilla chips
Soy Nuts (page 42)
Pickled Knackwurst (page 85)
Meatball Sandwiches (page 46)
Fudge Bars (page 53) *or*
Brownies
Beer

Before the game begins, set out the hot dip, crunchy soybean mixture, and the marinated knackwurst. Keep the dip warm in a fondue pot or chafing dish. When the players are ready for a break, serve the sandwiches and the bar cookies or brownies.

Make-a-Pizza Party (Serves 4)

Chili Pepper Pizzas (page 12)
Marinated Vegetable Snack (page 21)
Olive and Cheese Dip (page 39)
Potato chips   Vegetable dippers
Beverages

Move this party to the kitchen and let everyone choose their own pizza ingredients. Provide the vegetable snack and cheese dip for guests to nibble on while the pizzas bake.

Children's Picnic (Serves 12)

Butterscotch Crunch Sundaes (page 54)
Homemade Gumdrops (page 52)
Red Lollipops (page 26)
Chocolate milk or Lemonade

Set picnic tables with brightly decorated paper cloths and matching paper plates or napkins. Add old-fashioned candy jars filled with the lollipops and gumdrops.

Spur-of-the-Moment Party (Serves 4)

Curried Corn Snacks (page 41)
Cheese-Chili Burgers (page 46)
Relishes
Pickles
Apricot Fondue (page 8)
Angel cake dippers
Fruit dippers
Instant Russian Tea Mix (page 61) *for
iced or hot tea.*

Be prepared for short-notice guests by keeping
on hand the canned and packaged ingredients
called for in these recipes. To eliminate
hunting for items when making these snacks,
store the ingredients for each recipe
together in a plastic bag or corner of a cabinet.

Fondue Party (Serves 6)

Beer-Cheese Fondue (page 9)
French bread dippers
Vegetable dippers
Crunchy Meatball Fondue (page 11)
Sour cream dip with French onion
Chocolate-Butter Mint Fondue (page 6)
Apple dippers   Banana dippers
Beverages

Transfer cheese fondue and chocolate
mixture to fondue pots shortly before
serving; then, keep them warm over the
fondue burners. Remember to use a metal
cooker for the meatball fondue recipe.

Afternoon Tea (Serves 10)

Chicken Puffs (page 73)
Shrimp-Cucumber Rounds (page 70)
Buttered nut bread
Mixed nuts
Mints
Personality Pudding Tarts (page 31)
Lime-Frosted Punch (page 99)
Tea   Coffee

In warm weather consider serving iced tea as
a cooling beverage in place of hot tea.
Accompany the tea with cream or milk, sugar,
and lemon slices. To round out the tea
and other refreshments, serve the dainty and
colorful pudding tarts. To decorate
the tarts, use any of the suggested garnishes.

Appetizer Buffet (Serves 20)

Italian-Seasoned Gouda Spread (page 36)
Assorted crackers
Apple wedges
Classic Antipasto Tray (page 78)
Appetizer Pies (page 72)
Cheese Boreck (page 73)
Candied Orange Peel (page 26)
Chocolate-covered mint patties
Sunny Day Punch (page 99)
Coffee

Place appetizers throughout the room and
help avoid a pileup of guests at the buffet
table. For example, use an end table for
sweets, a desk for sandwiches, and a
narrow table behind the sofa for beverages.

Pre-Theater Party (Serves 6)

Appetizer Cheesecake (page 85)
Assorted crackers   Raw vegetables
Spicy Pineapple Chunks (page 64)
Harlequin Sandwiches (page 82)
Garlic-Buttered Shrimp (page 81)
Wine   Coffee

Invite theatergoers over for refreshments before the play begins. You can make most of the appetizers in this menu in advance, leaving you free to entertain when guests arrive.

Housewarming Party (Serves 6 to 8)

Pineapple-Orange Yogurt Dip (page 36)
Fruit dippers
Stuffed Cherry Tomatoes (page 62)
Date Roll-Ginger Snips (page 78)
Miniature Sesame Drumsticks (page 75)
Buttered Lemon Punch (page 101)
Hot or iced coffee

If you're a new homeowner or have just settled into a different apartment, throw a party to celebrate your move. Invite new neighbors as well as old friends to join in the fun.

Patio Party (Serves 8)

Anchovy-Cheese Ball (page 84)
Raw vegetables
Bacon-Crescent Roll-Ups (page 80)
Sweet-Sour Sausages (page 81)
Rosy Champagne Punch (page 96) *or*
Spicy Cranberry Punch (page 98)

Cook the brown-and-serve sausages on a hibachi or grill, and baste them with the sweet-sour mixture. Assemble the bacon-filled crescent roll-ups in a jiffy, and pop them into the oven to bake just as guests arrive.

After-the-Game Gathering (Serves 4 to 6)

Cucumber and Bacon Dip (page 36)
Vegetable dippers
Toasted Cereal Mix (page 42)
Caraway-Cheese Stack-Ups (page 45)
Pizza Muffins (page 14)
Tomato Beers (page 102)

Let guests snack on the dip, cereal mix, and cheese stack-ups while you assemble the tiny pizzas. Have plenty of the peppy beverage on hand for seconds. For a garnish, add a green onion stirrer to each glass.

Oriental Party (Serves 8)

Vegetables in Beer Batter (page 11)
Tiny Shrimp Rolls (page 80)
Teriyaki Appetizer Ribs (page 75)
Fortune cookies   Fresh fruit
Sake   Green Tea

Bring out the zucchini, cauliflower, and green pepper on round chopping blocks and slice them with a cleaver at the table. Have guests gather around an electric wok to fry their batter-coated vegetables.

Tree-Trimming Party (Serves 10 to 12)

Cranberry-Yogurt Dip (page 77)
Chicken, Turkey, or Ham dippers
Mosaic Sandwiches (page 68)
Chestnut Meatballs (page 75)
Sugar cookies
Gingerbread Men (page 28)
Mixed whole nuts
Eggnog (page 96)
Apple cider
Coffee

Children and adults of all ages will enjoy an evening of tree-trimming and carol-singing. Before guests arrive, unpack the tree ornaments and select Christmas music to play when decorating the tree. Include nut cracking in the festive activities. Provide nutcrackers and picks with the nuts.

Soup and Sandwich Buffet (Serves 10)

Lemon and Egg Soup (page 93)
Sherried Beef Broth (page 92)
Chicken Liver-Pimiento Rolls (page 73)
Shrimp-Cucumber Rounds (page 70)
Swiss-Olive Sandwiches (page 48)
Relishes
Camembert cheese
Fresh fruit
Coffee

Guests can fill their soup mugs and sandwich plates at the buffet table, then move to smaller tables to eat. Set the smaller tables with the silverware, napkins, and coffee mugs. When guests are ready for the cheese and fruit dessert, replace their sandwich plates with small dessert plates.

Informal Get-Together (Serves 6)

Triple Cheese Spread (page 39)
Assorted crackers
Marinated Fruit Combo (page 21)
Giant Pizza Sandwich (page 14)
Mixed drinks or
Carbonated beverages
Coffee

For the best results with mixed drinks, follow your recipes exactly. Use fresh fruit juices and peels, chilled or frosted glasses, shaved or chopped ice, and the size and shape of glass called for in the recipe.

Late-Night Party (Serves 8)

Chili Pepper Spread (page 39)
Assorted crackers
Split Pea-Cheese Fondue (page 9)
French bread dippers
Ham dippers
Bread Envelopes (page 18)
Scrambled eggs
Coffee
Wine

Invite friends over after the show or concert to discuss the night's events. While your friends are entertaining themselves, put the bread envelopes in the oven to heat and fix the scrambled eggs to fill the envelopes.

INDEX